BOOKS BY CECIL MURPHEY INCLUDE...

- **90** Minutes in Heaven
(with Don Piper)

- Gifted Hands: The Ben Carson Story
(with Dr. Ben Carson)

- The Spirit of Christmas
(by Cecil Murphey and Marley Gibson)

- Getting to Heaven: Departing Instructions
for Your Life Now *(with Don Piper)*

- Knowing God, Knowing Myself

- When a Man You Love Was Abused

- Hope and Comfort for Every Season

- Words of Comfort for Times of Loss

- Christmas Miracles
(by Cecil Murphey and Marley Gibson)

- When God Turned off the Lights

- When Someone You Love Has Cancer

- Everybody's Suspect in Georgia (fiction)

- I Choose to Stay and Immortality of Influence
(with Salome Thomas-EL)

- Rebel with a Cause *(with Franklin Graham)*

Real. Transparent. Honest. Gutsy. Straightforward.

UNLEASH
THE WRITER WITHIN

THE ESSENTIAL WRITERS' COMPANION

CECIL MURPHEY

OAKTARA

Waterford, Virginia

Unleash the Writer Within

Published in the U.S. by:
OakTara Publishers
P.O. Box 8, Waterford, VA 20197
www.oaktara.com

Cover design by Yvonne Parks at www.pearcreative.ca
Cover image © shutterstock.com: 33291877/Serhiy Kobyakov

Published in association with:
Deidre Knight of The Knight Agency, Inc., 570 East Avenue, Madison, GA 30650; http://www.knightagency.net/.

All Scripture quotations are taken from the Holy Bible, New Living Translation, copyright 1996, 2004, 2007 by Tyndale House Foundation. Used by permission of Tyndale House Publishers, Inc., Carol Stream, Illinois 06188, USA. All rights reserved.

ISBN: 978-1-60290-307-4

Printed in the U.S.A.

CONTENTS

1 • WHY DO YOU WRITE?

Why do you want to write? What pushes or compels you to keep on writing even though you receive rejection after rejection?

Those are the two major questions I've often asked writers at the more than 250 conferences where I've spoken or taught continuing classes over the past thirty-five years.

The conferees' responses vary, but the first ones usually begin with high-sounding tones—as if they want to please me, the teacher, or out of a desire to sound erudite. More than once someone has said, "I want to light the way for others to follow."

Another said, "I see writing as a high and holy occupation because we're committed to save the world from ignorance."

That's commendable—and maybe even true—but I knew those weren't the deepest reasons.

"I write to make sense of the world," one man insisted.

"Sounds profound," I said. "Perhaps a little too profound for me."

He added that he had so much chaos in his daily living that writing was one way he could make sense of his life. When I pushed him to explain further, he admitted he had read the statement in a book, liked it, and was satisfied with that as an answer.

A woman at a conference in Tennessee held up a laminated 3x5 card she kept in her purse. She said that the words, a quotation from Henry James, inspired her every time she read them. She later mailed me a copy:

> To live in the world of creation—to get into it and stay in it—
> to frequent it and haunt it—to think intensely and fruitfully—
> to woo combinations and inspirations into being by a depth and
> continuity of attention and meditation—this is the only thing.

I read the quotation many times before copying it here (with her permission). *The only thing?* That statement seems extreme, although I'm sure some people find the quotation inspirational. The words sound noble and probably inspire others, but they don't do anything for me. Perhaps I'm too much of a pragmatist.

To get beyond such lofty language, about five years ago I started opening my lectures this way: "Why do you want to write? While you think about your answer, I'm going to give you several reasons I write. After that, I'll listen to your responses."

As soon as they focused their attention on me, I said, "I write because I'm so full of myself, I believe the world is waiting to read my brilliant thoughts."

They laughed, a few nodded, and all seemed to know what I meant. I went on to explain that I also write because I'm driven to share my thoughts and insights on life.

"I'm a needy guy, and out of my need to feel appreciated, valued, and affirmed, I write," I say. "That's as simple and direct as I can put it. Our needs express who we are, what we lack, what we yearn for. All of us feel deficient in some ways."

I make one additional statement that seems to give several conferees the freedom to speak. "Writing is one way to compensate for my feelings of inadequacy."

The conferees relax. They no longer need to impress me with lofty statements. They're ready to give me gut-level responses.

Sometimes, to push them to think deeper, I add, "I write to resolve issues and explore possibilities. At times, it's a form of therapy. I've learned so much from my inward exploring, I've probably saved half-a-million dollars in therapist's fees by being a writer."

They usually laugh again.

Finally, before I allow them to respond, I write one sentence on the board or flip chart:

I write to find out who I am.

Then I wait.

The hands start waving, and they yell out the kind of things I like to hear. From my perspective, they finally speak from deep inside themselves. This is no longer an exam where they have to voice the right answer to please the teacher; they don't have to sound noble, sophisticated, or even spiritual.

Occasionally someone will say, "I want to have a book to use as a way to open up a public-speaking career."

That's certainly a legitimate answer.

Most of them, however, have deeply personal reasons for writing.

"I want to share what I know."

"I have things to say to enrich others."

"Writing broadens my life. The more I write and ponder," one man said, "the more I understand human nature, God, and the world in which I live."

"Writing satisfies my creative urge."

"I just have to do it!" one woman yelled. "Many times I tell myself I'll never write another word, but within a day or two I'm pounding the keyboard again."

It's interesting that "to make money" rarely appears on their list of reasons.

Why do *you* write?

"I write to find out who I am," is my primary answer. That may not be an obvious reason or one you'd yell out in my classes, but think about your reasons. You can't answer me, but you can answer yourself: Why do you write?

■ ■ ■

I know a man who often talks of writing novels, but he's been talking that way for at least a decade. Occasionally, he sets aside a Saturday and stays at his computer for one or two hours, but he hasn't produced anything significant.

I know this much about the man: His father wanted to be a writer but wasn't able to carry out his own dream. Is it possible that the son is trying to fulfill the dreams of the now-dead parent?

In his case, that may be behind his desire to write. Some children unconsciously live out the lives of their parents and don't know how to follow their own dreams.

Or perhaps my friend gets close to parts of himself that he's not willing to explore further. If so, I don't think he's conscious of it.

Your rational mind prevents your focusing on the real issues—the unresolved conflict you don't want to face. Your many activities and the demands of your job provide you with an abundance of excuses for not writing. You decide you're too involved in other, more urgent responsibilities so that writing becomes "something I want to do one day."

But someday isn't marked on your appointment calendar.

At one conference, a woman said, "I find fulfillment only in writing." And she extolled the virtues of writing hours every day.

That statement felt extreme to me. I'm not a therapist or a mind reader, but as I listened, I sensed that she used writing as a means to hide from life. By thrusting her energies into sharp dialog and intricate plots, she doesn't have to look at her otherwise chaotic life. It's an escape from life instead of an entrance into a healthier existence.

She chose the solitary life—and for years has spent most of her days in front of her computer, even though she has sold only a handful of articles. She is, however, highly active on Facebook, Linked-In, Twitter, and several writers' loops.

As I think about her, I assume it's her way to avoid participating in life's issues or to escape from other responsibilities.

That attitude doesn't trouble me, and she's not harming herself, but I believe her life would be richer if she pushed herself to work through her inhibiting issues.

I also have an acquaintance who has been working on one book for twelve years but has never finished it. "I'm polishing it," he'll say, or, "I've just had an idea on how to enhance the plot."

Is it possible he does that so he doesn't need to explain the lack of success in the rest of his life?

The above examples are only conjectures, but I hope you'll ponder them as you answer the question for yourself: *Why do I want to write?*

A therapist-friend said recently, "In Los Angeles, every waiter is a writer." He pointed out that would-be screenwriters feel drawn to such places, but he says it may be their way for having an excuse for not growing up. He believes many of them carry inside their heads the romantic image of the starving writer or creative person who doesn't fit into society.

Or do you want to write—really?

▪ I WRITE TO FIND OUT WHO I AM. ▪

2 - IS THIS YOUR GIFT?

At the end of the discussion in continuing classes at conferences, I make another point about why I write.

"I write because it is a gift."

Although it's difficult for me to say those words aloud, I believe I have an aptitude to communicate messages of encouragement on the page or screen. It's difficult to say because I don't want to come across as implying I have a special endowment that no one else does. Yet it's part of my "divine equipping," and I want to use it well.

I also have trouble expressing that God would favor me with such an endowment. Even now, after more than a hundred books, I'm still in awe that God would use *my* words to touch other people.

That sense of wonderment is the major reason I *know* it's a gift. Calling it a gift means it's not a possession I earned, nor is it an ability I produced by myself. It's a knack given to me for myself and for others.

My three brothers were gifted mechanics. They understood cars and could do things with them I couldn't understand. Others paint, learn languages, or play musical instruments. You may not see them as gifts, but you admit, "It's just something I can do."

Some of us have that innate ability with words—they flow from us. We express our thoughts easily and from our own style and personality. The ease of the language is characteristic of the gift.

Others try to write and may do so reasonably well, but their prose never has what I call the "ring" or sound of quality. I don't want to seem smug or condescending, but the ability to write and sell a book isn't, in itself, evidence of a gift.

From my early days of writing—even back in college—my instructors commented on how well I wrote. I had several classes under a long-tenured professor in graduate school, who told me, "You write excellent papers." I don't recall that he called it a "gift," but he told me how easy it was to read my papers. Even more important, he encouraged me to keep improving my skills. After I became a writer, he said, "I'm not surprised."

■ ■ ■

There's another element of a gift or talent—always learning and striving to improve. You may have an aptitude for writing, but what do you do about it?

You may not know if you're gifted because it's usually a matter of self-discovery. If you have that ability, you'll improve as you work at the craft—and you'll probably *want* to improve.

If it's not your talent, you'll plateau so that your writing will remain about the same year after year. Or you'll grow weary and quit.

Many years ago my wife and I took ballroom dancing classes and did extremely well. People often asked me if I was an instructor because I looked good on the floor. I had what they called a "good frame." I became fairly good, but never outstanding. One evening Shirley and I were dancing and I realized that I probably wouldn't improve much. I could learn new steps, but I would never be good enough to win the gold medal in a competition.

I accepted that. Although I enjoyed the movement and learned to stay in time with the music, I felt no compulsion, no drive, no intensity to push myself.

If you believe you have a gift to write, consider it the foundation on which you build. You still need to learn the skills to express what you want to say. Polish your grammar; learn good sentence structure. Those aren't automatic or part of the divine endowment: They're the skills gifted writers work to acquire. And if you don't have that flair, you'll never really get it.

Knowing you have a gift can do wonders for you. I'll explain it this way. In order to get into graduate school, I had to take a series of I.Q. and personality tests. When I returned for the read off, Dr. Bovee, the examiner, told me that I had scored high and shouldn't have trouble in my studies.

"I have one important question," I said. "I've always done well in school. When I was in college, my friend Al kept saying it was because I worked so hard." I explained that Al insisted my good grades weren't because I was bright, only that I put so much effort into my studies. "Was he right?" I asked.

Dr. Bovee laughed. "If you weren't smart, it wouldn't matter how hard you worked."

He said more, but that statement helped me immensely. I didn't feel I was smarter than others and I'm certainly not. But it did tell me (and my I.Q. score agreed) that I was intelligent. That was what I wanted to know. The knowledge of my intellectual ability gave me an immense boost of confidence in both of my graduate schools.

It works the same way when it comes to writing. To be able to admit, "I have the ability to write well" boosts my confidence. I know I can improve because I have the foundation of talent on which to build.

Like many others, for a long time I didn't recognize the ability as a gift—and I doubt that most writers do. We learn and appreciate our ability only as others respond to the words that come as a result of our labors.

Although I've written in the previous chapter about the reasons for writing, I still come back to one significant fact. If it's not part of your commitment and your divinely given talent, you won't pursue it: Write to find out who you are.

Writing isn't formal therapy, so you don't reach the place where you turn off your computer. Even though writing may have a therapeutic effect, you don't suddenly awaken to the reality that you write because you didn't get enough love in childhood and now you can focus on more appropriate ways to satisfy your yearning for affection. In therapy, you can probably get well enough to stop needing the sessions, but writing is different. Instead of stopping, you learn to feel your pain, write through your angst, grow through the lofty and low experiences and—if you stay at the craft—see it as an opportunity to enrich others.

The type of writing you do isn't crucial; it is essential that you discover the areas that touch your passion. You can learn and grow through writing novels, how-to books, curriculum, or instruction manuals. The genre isn't as important as what you put into it.

If you're a serious writer, like others, you hurt and sometimes the pain becomes intense as you touch parts of yourself that you'd prefer to ignore or deny. Serious scribes keep on writing anyway. Maybe it's because they have to, and it feels like compulsive behavior. Or maybe it's some kind of inner wisdom that whispers, "This is the way to wholeness."

I've often wondered if one of the reasons for the high level of alcoholism among successful writers doesn't center on their discovery of needs and inner hurts. They feel the pain and agony, but instead of facing their issues, they use alcohol or drugs to deaden their suffering.

One friend, who admits to being a highly insecure author of eleven books, says nothing gives him more joy than when he reads a good review of one of his books. "But then I sink into depression when I read a bad one."

When I asked why reviews affected him so strongly, he said in what I considered a rare moment of insight from him, "I have to have everyone's appreciation. If I think people don't like me, I get depressed." He held up his hand. "Okay, my writing and I are supposed to be separate, but they're not."

He had moved into the realm of self-discovery.

A woman who had published four sci-fi novels said, "In my most honest moments, I admit that I write to compensate for what I don't get in the real world. I can live a wonderful life through my fiction. I can write about my tragedies or my imagined ones and turn them into happy endings."

I don't want to discourage you from writing. If you understand the forces behind the burning desire to express yourself with words, you can become more productive and your manuscripts take on fuller meaning. Even if it's not a gift, you can still write and produce readable prose. You can also say to yourself, "I gave it my best."

Or you might stop writing.

Or worse, you might never start and always wonder if it was something you should have done. Some individuals are haunted by unconscious desires or needs that block a gift of creativity.

You may write for a variety of reasons. You may never fully understand your motives, but it's still a good question to ask yourself regularly: Why do I write?

The reasons vary, but they don't have to stop you. If you're truly a writer, you'll go deeper and your writing gets clearer.

▪ I WRITE BECAUSE IT'S MY GIFT. THE MORE I WRITE, THE MORE I KNOW WHO I AM. ▪

3 · BEING TRUE TO YOURSELF

What's wrong with being exactly who you are? Who says you have to morph into becoming someone else?

Too many read books by experts who suggest you should become different or urge you to become different. The pundits probably don't say you should remake yourself to become successful, but their instructions imply you're not good enough as you are.

If you heed their words, you may end up trying to be somebody you're not. To follow that advice not only weakens the power of your words, but the writing doesn't ring true because it no longer comes from deep within.

You can change, and most of us can, but you don't change much. And who says you have to become different? Those who pound out the message that you must constantly push yourself to be better, stronger, wiser, or healthier often imply a subtle, negative message: "You're inferior, but I can help you improve."

Here's the primary reason I push being real: *Everything you write reveals something about who you are—even your attempts at self-concealment.*

Your most honest writing becomes your best writing. Regardless of the genre, most experts say that all writing is autobiographical. In fact, everything you do is self-revealing.

If that's true, it follows that your best writing emerges as you become true to your inner convictions and increasingly open to who you are. No matter what your topic or genre, you always write about yourself—your values, your outlook, and your understanding (or lack of understanding) of the world in which you live.

It follows the adage that you write best what you know best. The better you know yourself, the higher the quality of your work. The better you know yourself, the more fully you understand and value human nature. As you probe within and more fully accept who you are and gradually understand your motives and core values, you strengthen and enrich your writing.

That concept hasn't always been clear to me. I remember the first time I grasped that fact. During my fourth week in graduate school, I walked down the street with my classmate Jerry Davis. We had been discussing how we reveal ourselves to others, often unintentionally.

"We constantly expose who we are," Jerry said. "We cannot *not* show ourselves by everything we do."

"Really?" I didn't disagree, but I simply hadn't thought along that line.

"Absolutely. We don't always interpret the information correctly, but the evidence is there." He spoke about such things as the clothes we wear, our hairstyles, our choice of cars, and the cadence of our speech.

As I listened to Jerry, I immediately resonated with his words. Now, years later, as a writer and a writing instructor, I realize how true this is in the writing profession.

Your word choices, your writing style, your voice, even the types of articles or books you read and those you write—everything— expresses who you are, intentional or not.

I saw this clearly during my early days of writing. One woman in our group was the wife of a minister and had a graduate degree in education. Her writing was technically correct, and I don't remember that we ever challenged her grammar.

Despite that, she was a bad writer. I use *bad* because her nonfiction wasn't authentic. It had the right tone and, in places, was insightful. But something was wrong. I finally figured it out and said, "You have a strong, professional voice."

She smiled.

"But it's not your voice."

Anger flashed in her eyes before she calmly asked, "What do you mean?"

"I know you and I like you. But you're not real on the page. You're a little too perfect and too wise."

Marion Bond West nodded in agreement. Marion was the most faithful member of the group and had just begun to publish with *Guidepost.* She said of the magazine, "They like stories about stumblebums—people who make mistakes and get things wrong."

I don't remember the rest of the conversation, but the woman never changed. Her writing showed her as being the epitome of wisdom. As far as I know, she never published a single article. In my opinion, she sought validation from us but was unable to give herself what she most needed.

I wish she had opened up and let us see her inner self on paper. One time she mentioned she had been adopted and, apparently, felt inferior and not as good as other people.

We weren't much help to her, but then she wasn't open to our assistance.

Like that woman, too many writers accept the subtle message that they're not good enough as they are. Perhaps you're one of them.

That means you feel defective. You don't think you can be successful or marketable unless you shed your true personality and search for formulas and magic techniques to transform yourself into something superior.

If there is one message I'd like writers to absorb, it's this:

You are acceptable as you are.

In the 1970s a bumper sticker caught my attention, and I've never forgotten the words: *God don't make no junk.* It's grammatically bad, but truthfully excellent. If God creates no junk, you do a great disservice to your creator and to yourself to infer or accept a label like *inferior quality* or *damaged goods.*

Many how-to books and workshops promise to deliver you from your negative and bad behavior and offer you amazing tips and powerful techniques—all to help you overcome your personal defects so you can write better. And you need to progress. We all do. But you don't improve if you negate who you are and hide yourself from your writing. If you accept such an implied message of being inferior, you constantly struggle to be somebody else who's superior.

- IF YOU FOCUS ON BEING DIFFERENT, HOW CAN YOU BE TRUE TO YOURSELF? AND IF YOU'RE NOT TRUE TO YOURSELF, WHO ARE YOU? -

4 · SEARCHING FOR THE REAL YOU

Like everyone else, you hold images of yourself—quite inaccurate ones—because you carry in your head your idealized self. This is who you think you are or are trying to prove that you are. It's as if there are two sides of yourself: the real and the idealized self.

Here are some of the things writers have said to me that helped me see the struggle between the real and the ideal and my unspoken response.

- "I'm a good writer." (If you are, let me tell you.)
- "I sell everything I write." (Really? Then you probably don't send out many manuscripts.)
- "All the editors praise my work." (You mean one editor liked your article.)
- "I've made back my advance on every book I've written." (Only about 20 percent of books earn back the author's advance.)

I wouldn't say that the above statements are lies, even though I put my response in parentheses. I consider them I-want-them-to-be-true statements. I see such statements as the idealized self speaking. It's who they want to be, who they work hard to become, but it's not who they really are.

Some would call that bragging, but I prefer to think of it as wishful or magical thinking.

None of the above quotations may be things you say about yourself. Yours may be different, but like all humans you have such thoughts because you want them to be true. They're not declarations or announcements made after careful analysis, but words that pop out of your mouth.

When I was a boy, there was a short pudgy comedian, whose name I can't remember. He used to make optimistic statements, often ridiculous, and almost *soto voce* added, "I hope. I hope. I hope." This sounds flat on paper, but people laughed every time. I sometimes think of him when people give outlandish testimonies about their abilities or achievements.

Many writers also carry inside them bad images of themselves as writers and of their talent. Both might be true—the inflated ideas of ourselves and the less-than-true feelings or words.

- "I'm not much of a writer."
- "No one will ever want to read anything I write."
- "I'm kidding myself if I think I can sell this."
- "My style is too simplistic (or too flowery, or I use too many words, or I don't use enough words)."
- "I'm kidding myself if I think I have something to say."

You may be a person who flits from one extreme to the other. Sometimes you're the best writer since Moses chiseled out the Ten Commandments; other times, you wonder how you could entertain the grandiose idea that anyone would read your junky, mangled manuscripts.

As you learn and mature, the real and the idealized (or the real and negative ideal) gradually move closer together. You learn who you are, which implies self-acceptance. You not only write more authentically, but your writing becomes stronger, more confident, and truer to the person you're becoming.

One question, however, presents a serious problem and one to which you need to find an answer in the search for the real you:

Whom do I wish to please?

That sounds simple, and it's easy to provide a hasty answer and move on. Please don't do that, because it's not effortlessly answered.

To sell any piece of writing, you have to please an editor or an agent. That means your writing can't be self-indulgent and focused on anything that happens to pop into your head.

For instance, years ago, I tried to encourage a writer. I read a short piece he wrote. The language was beautiful, although he piled on one image after another for about six hundred words.

"You write beautifully," I said, "but what does it mean? I can't understand what you're trying to say."

"You have to figure out the meaning," he said. "I write to force people to think."

"*I think* you'll never sell it."

We stayed in touch for perhaps five years, and he didn't change. He didn't sell either.

The question is even more relevant if you try to sound like "a real writer." Too many want-to-be-successful authors get the idea that you must write in a certain way to succeed.

This trend shows itself to me when I read certain romance genres. "They read as if they all have the same ghostwriter," I said to one of my friends. Although an exaggeration, it was obvious that they copied each other's styles, used the same heavy-handed words, and included the same clichés. It's as if they said, "It worked for her, so it must be good or she wouldn't be published."

My response is, "Maybe she got published in spite of her lack of craft."

Discovering your voice (more on that in later chapters) is part of that process. Yet it's more than that. I'm talking about *discovering yourself.* About learning who you are, accepting who you are, and affirming yourself.

I'm tired of reading those who try to impress me with their knowledge, learning, or tell me more about the Greek aorist tense than anyone cares to know. If the previous sentence sounds exaggerated, I can assure you it's not. Some scribes become fascinated with a topic and can't seem to leave it alone.

And I want to add my personal confession.

I once wrote a novel in which the plant pyrethrum was a

significant factor in the storyline.[1]

I began my research and enjoyed what I learned. In my first draft I had nearly four pages about the plant and the industry. Even I realized it was too long, so I cut and ended up with slightly more than two pages. By the time I sent in the manuscript I had five paragraphs. My wise editor condensed it to a single paragraph. That was an invaluable lesson for me.

Here's a question I asked myself: "Who will miss this information if it's not there?"

One man who joined one of my writing groups, the Scriptiques, wrote a two-thousand-word article on *kai*. That Greek word, nearly always translated "and" doesn't need clarification. He went into lengthy paragraphs about what the apostle Paul meant when he used *kai* and how it differed from the way John, James, and Peter used it.

After I finished reading the article, I wrote two words at the bottom: *So what?*

My response may sound harsh, but he spent his energies on a topic so esoteric that none of us cared. Two of us had studied New Testament Greek. Another member of the group nicely suggested he write on "words with a little more substance."

This isn't to judge that man, but I felt he was hiding among his words and unwilling to let us know who he was. I assumed that he idealized himself (or wanted to be considered a scholar) to receive our applause and admiration.

Do you want to be authentic? If not, close this book. It's not for you.

Do you want to present the real you and not settle for the ideal or your fantasized self? It's not an easy task, and it's a lifetime effort.

Maybe you'll never quite become the **real** you, but you can get closer. Here's how I said it at a recent conference: "When I write, I don't want people to read me and not like me for who I am not; I

---

[1] Pyrethrum is a natural herbicide, originally from Japan, but grown in other countries such as Kenya.

want people to like me for who I am. They may not like my writing; they may not like the person who wrote, but at least they will have encountered the real me."

Most of us tend to resist finding our real selves. Sometimes we're afraid we won't like the person we meet at the end of the journey. One man said, "I might discover there was nobody there." (He was wrong, but I understood.)

In my own writing, I struggle with doubts, questions, anxieties, probably no worse than many others. But I keep on. I pursue the illusive self.

Does any of this sound like you?

Ultimately, my response to the question about whom I wish to please is simple: I want to please myself. I do that in context. That is, I want to provide my literary agent with manuscripts she can get excited about and enthusiastically sell. I want enough substance and style that I can make an editor smile. If I do that, and it comes from deep within myself, I know it's right, regardless of the sales.

If that happens, it means I'm a few steps closer to finding out who I really am. The more I discover who I am, the more I'm able to embrace myself. The best part of this is the ultimate result of my work. If my writing is the best and most authentic I know how to make it, it's good writing.

Good writing.

Not perfect. Just good.

That doesn't mean everyone or anyone will like it. You'll probably still get rejections (which I do) but you'll know you've found the real you. That's more important than all the success you can achieve.

■ ■ ■

About a month before Hitler executed him, Dietrich Bonhoeffer wrote a poem translated into English as "Who Am I?"

He asks that question several times and presents two pictures of himself. Some see him as one who bears "the days of misfortune equally, smilingly, proudly, like one accustomed to win."

He also asks:

Or am I only what I know of myself, restless and longing and sick…weary and empty at praying, at thinking, at making, faint and ready to say farewell to it all?

He again asks himself who he is:

This or the other? Am I one person today, and tomorrow another? Am I both at once? A hypocrite before others, and before myself a contemptibly woebegone weakling?

He concludes with these three sentences:

Who am I? They mock me, these lonely questions of mine.
Whoever I am, Thou knowest, O God, I am thine.

I wish I were brilliant enough to have come up with those lines, but I certainly affirm them.

> ■ I MAY NEVER FULLY KNOW THE REAL ME,
> BUT I SEARCH FOR MY TRUE SELF.
> I LEARN MANY LESSONS ON THE JOURNEY. ■

5 · THE CONCEIT OF WRITING

E.B. White once said it took courage to write and "even a little conceit." And it does. I've jokingly said earlier in this book that I'm so full of myself I think the world can hardly wait to read me. On one level that's true.

That doesn't mean it's painless or easy. Nothing I've ever done has tormented me more than writing. At times the stress level has become almost unbearable, especially when I've faced a self-imposed deadline. I take my blood pressure almost every morning, but I usually know when it's going to read higher than normal: When I'm uptight because the writing doesn't flow, or the words gush out but they're crooked and tangled and different from the way they sounded inside my head.

Despite that, I've earned my living at writing for nearly thirty years, and I can't think of anything I would rather do even if I lived to be 150. I may grumble a little, or ask myself, "Why did I agree to do this project?" or "I must have been nuts to sign that contract."

Yet I keep on. I don't give up.

If I write a five-hundred-word article, I'm making a claim about myself. I'm saying I know things others don't. Or I tackle an old topic with a different perspective and experience new understanding. I examine old ideas and discover new meaning or inferences that others have bypassed.

Isn't that conceit?

It certainly is.

Or let's try the negative side. If I write badly and everyone knows it, I lose face. And for some of us, that's the worst punishment—being ridiculed or rejected by our peers.

For instance, a British woman wrote a novel, which I never read.

It was her second book and both were ebooks that sold on Amazon for $1.99, which made them inexpensive reads. The owner of one blog reviewed her second novel, pointed out misspelled words on almost every page and occasional slips of grammar. Despite that, he said she showed promise, encouraged her, and implied that others should download her book.

The woman apparently grabbed on only to the negative things, because she wrote a scathing rebuttal. Several readers of the blog read her comments and responded heatedly. Each was less kind than the original review.

She argued with every posting and claimed to have two versions on Amazon and insisted they must have downloaded the wrong one. Bad move. Several people downloaded both versions and said the typos and grammar were as bad on either.

Before the end of that one day, more than three hundred people posted comments about her ebook (both versions), and not one was positive. Worse, they excoriated her for her lack of professionalism in defending herself. Several of them claimed to have wasted $1.99.

The blog responses went viral, and I received the URL from someone, who thought it was the funniest thing she had read in months. I agreed that, on one level it was funny, but it was also extremely sad.

One agent described the British novelist as the personification of "the client from hell."

Once it went viral, the postings escalated and the novelist's language turned crude and vulgar. The blogger finally said, "No more posts," and that ended the furor.

I mention this because I've thought of that poor woman many times. I read enough of her paragraphs through the postings that I could see she needed a good editor.

She was probably ignorant of good writing and unwilling to learn or perhaps unable to pay for an editor. Even given those possibilities, think of the conceit—the self-elevated concept of her abilities. Whether she really believed in her immense talent, as she said in more than one post, or she was trying to convince herself and readers isn't germane.

That woman exceeded the limits to which most of us would go on our own behalf, but that also makes my point.

As a writer, you need a certain amount of conceit to write and send out a manuscript. Even if you're doubtful and fearful, it means you're still arrogant enough to believe you have insight that someone else doesn't have. Or you have a novel with a plot that no one else has written or hasn't written it as cleverly, or you have so many twists that no one could possibly identify the guilty party until the end of the book.

That's conceit.

That's also part of a writer's makeup. And it's all right to acknowledge it.

If you write, it speaks of your sense of self-importance and pride. That's being honest, and that's not bad.

For some, the writing journey is a conscious (or unconscious) search to figure out who you are. I raise my hand on that one.

Years ago someone asked me why I wrote in so many different genres. Part of my answer is that I wrote on topics I don't know or understand. I wrote to gain a better understanding of the world and of myself. At that point, "understanding of myself" was almost a tag-on. Today, I'd start with that phrase.

Someone said, "I'm rewritten by what I write." That states it well, and it's my goal. That statement means that, at its best, writing is self-discovery.

I would like the words of this book to help, encourage, exhort, and entertain you. I yearn for all writers (including you) to accept their ambition and conceit, and I want to help. In the process, however, remains the deep-seated search to know who you are and to be more aware of your motives and attitudes.

So call it *conceit,* and it is, but I truly hope it's not self-indulgence. I also hope I'm not what therapists term narcissistic.[2]

---

[2] Havelock Ellis coined the word, based on the Greek myth of Narcissus, a handsome, self-absorbed young man who fell in love with his own reflected image in a pool. Most therapists consider that some narcissism is part of our essential makeup, and we need it to live a healthy, balanced life.

By contrast, every once in a while writers approach me at conferences and tell me about their books. "It is so deep," they say and start telling me about their understanding as if they expect me to swoon and gasp, "That's the most profound thing I've heard in my life."

I wish I could respond that way.

As I listen, or when I read their prose, I don't say so, but I think, *Where's the depth? This is information almost everyone knows. Why would you think it's profound?*

I can't speak for them, but my sense is that because it came to them as a revelation or an insightful moment, they perceive that it's more mysterious and multilayered than the thoughts of others.

There's another significant factor. Along with the self-absorption or conceit must be a burning drive. It has to be that inner force that cries out, "I have to do this. I have to write! I have to see my words on the screen or page."

From my perspective, there are few problems with writing. Anyone of normal intelligence can learn the craft. The problems are human. Much of what writers may refer to as "writing problems" are problems within themselves. They think too highly of themselves, or they see themselves as too lowly; they fear being honest, lack courage, or are unable to face what they might learn about themselves.

E.B. White once said the major problem of writers was that they had to establish communication with themselves. If they could communicate, others would respond.

Here's how I say it: If I articulate well the things that seem the most personal and the most intimate, they become the most common and the most universally understood.

On a different topic, the apostle Paul makes a similar point when he writes, "The temptations in your life are no different from what others experience."[3] I don't know the context out of which he wrote, but I assume there were individuals who felt the lure to do wrong was unique to them and that no one else faced the extreme enticement

---

[3] 1 Corinthians 10:13a

over which they struggled.

They were wrong.

Their temptations themselves were always the same, but the attitude and the enticement was (and is) common to every human being.

■ I AM CONCEITED ENOUGH TO WRITE. I AM ENTHUSIASTIC ENOUGH TO BELIEVE I HAVE THINGS TO SAY. ■

6 · LIKING YOURSELF

Instead of seeking to modify and reshape your personality, I plead with you to accept, value, and nurture yourself. Why don't you become more fully who you already are? In the process, you mature, and your writing improves.

To carry this further, doesn't it make sense that the better you know yourself, the better you write? Thus, the more honestly you write, the closer you come to knowing who you really are.

As you seek to write better, the effort also becomes part of the search for greater self-understanding. The corollary is that the more fully you accept yourself, the less you censor or block your writing flow, and the better you produce words that touch others.

Some writers, however, are afraid of discovering who they are and won't open that door of exploration. Here's my position, and I state it in several ways in this book: To excel at the craft, you need to learn skills and techniques. Just as much (perhaps more) you need to understand as much as you can about the source of your writing—yourself.

For the past decade, I've encouraged writers to value their uniqueness. As I do with them, I urge you to embrace your divinely given personality and ability, get excited about your uniqueness, and use that knowledge to make yourself an increasingly effective writer.

Although you need to acquire skills to do your job efficiently, you also need to honor your ability (no matter how little you think you have) and enjoy being who you are. Perhaps your weaknesses may not be the negatives you think they are.[4]

---

[4] In Chapter 9, I write about the relationship between our gifts and our weaknesses.

If you learn to capitalize on who you *are* and appreciate *who* you are, you're on your way to becoming the best writer you can become.

■ ■ ■

Sometimes I ask writers two significant questions:

- What would it do to your writing if you could appreciate yourself as you are and see that your weaknesses are as important as your giftedness?

- How would it affect your writing if you weren't constantly looking at your faults but focusing on what you can do?

Silence often fills the room while they ponder their response.

To make the best use of your abilities as a writer, start with healthy self-valuing and the affirmation of your gifts. As you appreciate yourself, you learn to like yourself, and that knowledge becomes both powerful and empowering.

I don't advocate rigid self-discipline. I tried that. For years, I held to tight schedules, refused to allow deviations, and castigated myself when I failed. I've since learned that true self-discipline flows out of gentleness and self-respect.

I'll illustrate what I mean. People call me transparent, real, and honest. And I'm getting more that way all the time. I haven't always been vulnerable on paper. During my first years of writing, my initial attempts were a bit pompous and condescending.

Many years ago, Charlotte Hale, a professional writer in my first editing group, the Scribe Tribe, said to me, "If you're going to be successful, you must be willing to walk down the street naked."

I don't know if that was original with her, but the message stayed with me. If I close my eyes, I can see her sitting across the table, leaning slightly toward me. She smiled before she spoke those words.

I heard them as divinely given revelation. I've often said that sentence was the single best piece of advice I ever received about my role as an author. Immediately my work improved.

I continue to strive for that metaphorical nakedness when I write. I continue to move toward an appreciation of myself and the writing process. Creating readable prose isn't something I need to bully or shame myself into doing. My best writing comes when I treat myself compassionately and caringly. Part of that is to accept the less-than-wonderful parts of myself.

If writers bully their fragile egos, they often get the results they want—and I write that statement from experience—but they won't like themselves.

Healthy self-discipline grows out of liking who you are and encouraging your desire to be even better.

Only by knowing who you are and compassionately embracing yourself can you grow as an individual and as a writer. If you *relentlessly* pursue self-understanding, accept your own experiences as authentic, and are willing to compose from that truer, deeper part of yourself, you generate the kind of writing that comes across as authentic. Honest. True.

Another way to say it is that as you accept, respect, and trust yourself, it becomes easier to accept, respect, and trust *your writing*.

> **▪ THE BETTER I KNOW MYSELF,**
> **THE BETTER I WRITE.**
> **THE BETTER I LIKE MYSELF,**
> **THE BETTER WRITER I BECOME. ▪**

7 ▪ YOUR INNER CRITIC

The first days of pushing to become published almost became my last. I felt as if two voices screamed at me—at the same time—and pounded my brain with contradictory messages. One way to explain this to myself is to use the dichotomy of right brain versus the left brain.[5]

The two adversaries warred against each other and neither respected the other. My right brain, filled with wonderful, exciting, creative ideas nudged me. "Go for it, Cec. Great stuff. I love it. You can do it. Yes! Yes!"

The left brain snarled and tapped my shoulder. "This is garbage. No one will ever want to read this. Why would an editor pay you money for this tripe?"

I fought my negative voice, but the more I fought it, the louder the interior volume. I wrote; I published articles; the voice screamed, but I kept on. I sold my first book and three more after that, but additional sales didn't stop the incessant screaming inside my head.

I read the experts to see what they said. I spoke with a few top-selling authors. It was gratifying to know that others fought the same battle, but their solutions left my head shaking in confusion and amazement. My writing critic never shut up.

I didn't know the answer, and I wasn't sure they did either, but I kept searching. "Silencing the Inner Critic" is the title of a chapter of a book I picked up recently. The writing instructor advised students to yell, "Shhh" or "Shut up!" when that disquieting voice interfered with the writing flow. He also offered them several techniques they could

---

[5] I use right brain, left brain as a point of illustration, although many call this distinction into question.

use to silence that voice. He insisted that if they denied the existence of that critical scream , they didn't have to listen.

Shut up the voice? Deny its existence? The more I thought about such advice, the more I disagreed.

- What if that inner editor isn't totally bad?
- What if that inner critic wants to be my friend and not my enemy?
- What if the critic has something valuable to say?
- What if that voice is correct? largely correct? only a quarter correct?
- Is it possible that I need to listen to the carping and yelling instead of fighting and arguing?

Others suggest you gently ignore your inner editor—don't argue but continue on as if there's no sound. That's only slightly different from the other advice.

Think about what such advice really means: ignoring or pushing aside parts of yourself that you don't like. Ignoring these parts doesn't work—or at least it's not a productive procedure. When I've tried that technique, the voice becomes even more insistent. It's like the person who stands with a finger on my doorbell and won't stop ringing it until I open the door.

Those internal critics are clever, and they'll find a way to make you hear their voices. They won't be ignored, or at least not forever. That approach to the inner critic makes me think of individuals who jump on to the latest fad diet. They soon learn everything they can't eat, and they push aside those foods. Deprivation works at first, but finally the body rebels and says, "I'm going to eat. In fact, I'll show you! I'll demand even more food this time!"

Ignoring isn't the answer, and as I learned, it refused to silence itself.

Some experts say you need to separate the creator and the internal censor. Give yourself space to explore, think, feel, and express. They say you do that by tuning in to another channel in your brain.

But is that a good idea? Isn't ignoring it like denying or being ashamed of such a voice?

Other experts will urge you to find ways to "appease" the censor. I used to have a book in my library with a chapter called "Making Peace with Your Inner Critic." The author said that, instead of pushing away the demanding voices, you need to release them—to let them go. He spent a dozen pages to point out that inner critics are unsatisfied parts of yourself and that, as you accept yourself, you can just release those voices. Although that advice didn't seem right, at least he was a step beyond silencing the noise.

Another instructor urges writers to pause and write exactly the words their inner critic speaks. If that helps, then do it. That seems quirky to me and I think it detracts, leads you off the path, and may hinder your creativity.

Here's where I stand today: I don't believe in ignoring the internal editor; I do believe there is a time to listen to it.

If you're open to every part of yourself—and I hope you will be—you can teach your right brain and your left to hug each other and work in harmony.

Here's how I figured this out. In 1989 a publisher contracted with me to ghostwrite the autobiography of Dr. Ben Carson of Johns Hopkins Hospital. I enjoyed working with Ben in a motel room in Baltimore and getting the data from him. It was unquestionably the fastest, smoothest interviewing I'd ever done.

Afterward, I flew home to Atlanta and began to write. For the first six chapters, my right brain cheered me on. "This is wonderful. You're getting it! Yes, this is good stuff!"

In the middle of Chapter 7, something shifted inside my head. The inner critic had remained silent, but then he whispered, "This isn't really bad—I mean, it doesn't stink, but it's not that good."

I mentally screamed, "Get thee behind me, Satan," and kept on writing.

After that experience, the writing didn't flow as rapidly and the critical voice said *soto voce*, "It's getting worse. You're going downhill."

For the next five or six chapters, the critical voice grew more insistent. My typing slowed, and my creative powers numbed, but I kept on. "They'll demand that you return the advance," the voice threatened. "They'll never ask *you* to do another book."

The battle raged, but I kept on. I was stubborn, and I reminded myself that I had a contract and an ethical obligation to complete the book, no matter how badly it turned out.

The day came when I finished the full draft. I sighed, shut off my computer for a day, and groaned about the miserable writing job I had done.

For two days I kept trying to figure out what I could do to salvage the mess I had made of the wonderful story of Dr. Ben Carson. Finally, I decided that the only thing I could do was to sit in front of my computer and start the repair job—if it wasn't already beyond that.

After I turned on my computer, I began to read my material as I started the revision. Now that I had a full manuscript, I gave my inner editor total freedom to change anything. "It's okay," I told myself. "Be as critical, mean, and as hard as you want. Let's make this a good book."

My internal censor went to work. I caught a bad sentence or a place where I used the same word four times in a single paragraph. I rewrote an occasional sentence.

To my surprise, I couldn't find the places my inner critic had screamed about so loudly. I found weak spots—many of them—and places I needed to clarify or a few paragraphs where I had gotten too technical or too verbose in a particular section.

By the time I had finished the revision, I said, "Hmm, this wasn't as bad as I had thought. It's not perfect, and I need to do more work on it, but it's not complete garbage."

The day came when I finished Ben Carson's autobiography called *Gifted Hands* and sent the full manuscript to my editor. It has been published by HarperCollins, Zondervan, and Review and Herald. Since 1990, the book has sold in excess of four million copies in English and about forty other languages. It's still available in hardback, trade paper, and mass paper. In 2010, Johnson & Johnson presented the film version on TNT starring Cuba Gooding Jr., and it followed the book quite closely. Next to *90 Minutes in Heaven,* it's the best-selling book I've ever written.

What did I learn from that experience?

First, I couldn't trust my emotions on the good or inferior level of my writing while I was in the process.

Second, I decided I needed to listen to every part of myself. Let that voice speak! The critic sounded like a tyrant, but perhaps it was tired of being pushed around. Once I allowed both sides of my brain to function, I felt more at peace and open.

I now listen to my internal wisdom. Why consider the internal editor an enemy or a nuisance? Why not engage that part as a helper? Why fight a part of myself that wants to help?

It still took a long time before I could consider that voice as a friend—but that came in time. Now I trust and honor the left part of my brain as much as I do the right side.

- MY INNER CRITIC CAN BE MY FRIEND, SO I HONOR AND TRUST THAT VOICE. -

8 • HONORING YOUR INTERNAL CRITIC

L et's think some more about that censorious voice. For example, when you were small, you developed a conscience or a voice that said, "Fire burns. Don't touch." "If you jump off the top step, you'll get hurt." You listened (or didn't), and today you know those warnings are correct.

That influence is constantly with you and never stops working. Its purpose is to keep you safe. In childhood, safety meant not getting hurt; in maturity, safety focuses on protective, inner issues.

Isn't it possible that the insistent editor in your writing may be doing the same thing for you that your conscience does? The criticism may not always be correct, but it deserves your attention.

What if your persistent voice truly wants to give you helpful information and guidance? What if it *doesn't* want to hinder you?

Some internal voices may be timid, fearful, and too cautionary; they don't want you to take big risks. But that doesn't mean you ignore them. You may have to talk to that part of yourself—to assure yourself that it's all right to keep going.

Many can't seem to make peace with that interior editor and struggle endlessly. When I feel the conflict going on inside my head, I say one sentence to myself. Occasionally, I have to say it several times, but it works: "I write creatively, and I edit analytically."

My friend Steven James says it this way: "I write hot, but I edit cold."

In the film, *Finding Forrester*, the Pulitzer-prize winning author named Forrester advised the young man to write the first draft from his heart and the second from his head.

At some spot in writing, a piece may not flow well. That's when the internal critic starts to hum the funeral dirge.

"You may be correct in the things you want to show me," I tell my insistent interrupter (and I say it aloud), "but you can't interfere until I have something on the screen for you to criticize." That logic usually works.

If the voice persists, I pause and talk calmly—I really do this. "I understand your need to be ruthless in letting only quality writing leave my desk. I admire you for caring that much and for that serious commitment, but right now, relax. Allow my creative side to write and get everything prepared for your inspection. Once it's written, you can have fun, while you slash, cut, and delete as much as you like."

I'm fair to both of my voices. For me it works, because both parts of me like to know that I don't play favorites.

"Vomit on the screen."

That's how I advise my students. "Let go and write as rapidly as you can. This is especially true in the beginning stages of your career. If you keep your fingers moving, you don't have as much negative internal chatter."

After you finish the first draft of a story, article, or chapter, you're ready to negotiate with your critical editor. "Now, you may have your turn. Read, criticize, and edit as much as possible. I promise to listen to you, because I know you want me to produce quality writing."

Such an attitude shows respect and affirmation for that censorious part of yourself.

That's the third thing I learned: *To treat myself compassionately.* I still struggle with doubts,[6] but I don't usually have to fight the voice that says my stuff is stupid, badly written, or illogical.

---

[6] See Chapter 19, "Because I Was Afraid."

On the occasions when I feel that way, I say to that voice, "If that's true, you're going to have a lot of work to do when your turn comes." Most of the time, I don't have to go that far.

Over the years of writing professionally, I've learned to speak kindly to my critical self. As I've implied, I wasn't always compassionate toward Cec. In the first years of writing, I demanded, pushed, and pleaded that the analytical segment of my brain stop bothering me. Now I enjoy writing as a wonderful collaboration between the creative, intuitive part of my brain and the analytical, critical side.

Finally, here's the biggest discovery I made—which sounds simple but it was quite revolutionary for me: *It's much easier to edit a page of writing than it is to edit a blank screen.*

Or try it logically (which appeals to my left-brained critic): *How can I invite my critical faculties to function until my creative writer has written something?*

The first step in good writing is to get something written. It's all right to tell the critic to wait—provided you give that part of yourself equal time. "Be polite to all parts of yourself," I once said in a workshop. "Your right side has to go first, because it has something to say."

To your left side you can say, "Relax. You have to wait for your turn. You may not interrupt, but you'll wait silently until your counterpart has finished because you have good manners. After your counterpart is finished, you have total permission to go behind me and tear up as much of his work as you like."

My inner critic doesn't smile when I talk that way (he doesn't know how), but he doesn't argue. He's satisfied as long as I give him the opportunity to voice his opinion and I listen.

Because of the cooperation of both parts of myself, I write with greater passion and creativity.

These days when that irritating voice speaks to me, I stop writing and talk gently to myself. "It's all right. Today you're feeling a bit anxious or insecure, but if you'll be patient and let me finish, I'll help you slash as much of the manuscript as you like. "

For me it works.

**▪ I WRITE CREATIVELY,
AND I EDIT ANALYTICALLY. ▪**

9 · WEAKNESSES—OR GIFTS?

Three of us went to a booksigning of an author we knew slightly. He was a man we wanted to encourage by our presence and by each of us buying a copy of his latest book.

We arrived early, so two of us looked around. Rick stood at the cash register and talked with the clerk until the author arrived. He moved out of the way each time a customer came to the counter.

I overheard him say, "I'm writing a novel."

"What's it about?" she asked, which was a natural question.

Rick told her by starting at the first page and going through the story. A few minutes later, I passed by again. Because I knew his novel (and had heard the storyline at least twice), I realized Rick was almost at the midpoint. The woman tried to look neutral, but her hands fidgeted.

I smiled at her, hoping it said, "I'm sorry for what you're going through."

After nearly fifteen minutes, the author arrived and, to Rick's credit, he hurried to the ending and joined the rest of us to greet the author.

An hour later as we drove away, Rick said, "I told the saleswoman that I was writing a novel, and she wanted to know the whole plot." He went on to tell us that she said it sounded wonderful and was sure he'd be successful.

Rick never sold the novel, but that's not why I relate this story. He needed affirmation—a lot of affirmation.

By then I had known Rick for about two years. If his friends didn't praise him, he had a number of ways to heap laurels on himself.

I was aware of a childhood in which he felt he was never good enough. No matter what he did, his father made him feel as if he had failed and should have done better.

Here's another example. A woman writer, who has probably published twenty books in the past two decades, is much like Rick. She sells more, but she's as needy as he is. Her books are all right, but I sense she hides behind her words.

I'm not a therapist, and I hope my writing doesn't sound as if I'm trying to imitate one. My sense of the woman is that she's so afraid of criticism that who she is never comes out on the pages. Her mediocre writing could be better, but I don't think she could handle negative reviews.

When she speaks and writes, she patronizes readers, although I sense she's unaware of her tone. Again, I see it as her neediness. If she comes across as the authority, no one can argue with her. She constantly writes, "You must..." or, "It is important to..." By themselves the two statements don't sound bad, but in context, she uses them as if she's an authoritarian schoolteacher admonishing eight-year-old girls.

In these two examples I've presented two needy, negative-impact individuals. Their inner privation shows in what they write.

But then, all of us express our neediness in what we write. I used those two examples because they seem obvious.

■ ■ ■

Think about your different strengths and weaknesses. Let's start with the premise that the two terms are opposite sides of the same issue. Your power is also your drawback.

Here's how it works with me. One of my strengths is *clarity*. When people read my writing, I don't want them to ask, "What does that mean?" (I didn't say I was perfect at this, but it is something for which I strive.)

I earned two undergraduate degrees and two graduate degrees and finished a year's work on my doctoral degree. I mention that because one concern is that I don't want to lose what someone calls the common touch. I want to reach audiences with high school education and yet be able to speak on a level that educated people can enjoy reading.

A few people have called that a *weakness* and refer to "his simplistic style." They are correct, although I like the word *simple* better than *simplistic*.

Consider another factor: I'm extremely transparent—and that's on purpose. Here's a saying I wrote years ago and repeat it regularly:

I would rather be disliked for who I am than to be admired for who I'm not.

If you read several pieces of my writing, or just finish this book, you'll catch my *vulnerability* (which is the other word people use about me). It's a gift and adds potency to my writing.

But the other side of transparency is also true: I may self-reveal more than readers care to know. My favorite illustration of that is about the boy who went to the library and wanted a book about penguins for a report.

The librarian showed him a shelf of about thirty books and said, "They're all on that topic."

A few minutes later the boy walked away from the shelf and said to the librarian, "That was more about penguins than I wanted to know."

Translated into clear language, it means I wonder sometimes if I reveal more than people are interested in reading.

In the late 1990s, I wrote the first book of my own in a decade. For ten years I had only ghostwritten for other people. A major factor is that I didn't value my voice or the quality of my work.

I finally wrote a manuscript, and my agent placed it with an enthusiastic editor. However, she became so overwhelmed with other projects that demanded more of her time than she had allotted, so the publisher outsourced the project.

A freelancer edited the manuscript and sent back the first three chapters. My first sentence went this way: "Sometimes prayer bores me, and I wonder why I do it; sometimes prayer excites me, and I know why I do it."

She changed it to: "Prayer, at its best, is an intimate conversation with God." She virtually rewrote those three chapters so I would have a model for rewriting the rest of the book.

She sent this note along: *This doesn't belong in print. It's the kind of thing you need to put in your personal journal.*

I complained to the editor and to the vice-president, whom I'd known for years. "If it was good enough for acceptance the way I wrote it, why is it no longer good enough?"

They fired the freelancer, and I waited three months for the original editor. That story has a happy conclusion, but the point is that not everyone likes my writing style or is comfortable with my gut-level honesty.

That's a risk I've chosen to take.

Here's one more area of my giftedness. I write with *heart.* I've heard that term from editors since the early days of my writing career. *And it is a gift.*

I often tell students, "I can teach techniques, but I can't teach heart. I can encourage you to open up, but you must be willing to show your true self on the page."

In writing the two paragraphs above, I'm also using it to explain and accept a great need in my life. I had little encouragement as a child. I won't say my parents didn't love me; I will say I can't think of a single instance of feeling loved by them. After I had become "professionally acceptable," I received their approval, even their admiration. They bought copies of my books for friends. But I never felt their love.

Because of my inborn need to be cared about, to yearn for parental affection and not receive it, I sought acceptance and affirmation elsewhere. For example, school was a marvelous place for me, because I realized that the teachers liked me and gave me the kind of encouragement I didn't receive from my parents.

Although I didn't perceive this fact for years, I also sought love by giving what I wanted to receive. It's easy for me to reach out to the hurting. I left the professional pastorate in 1984, but my wife insists that I'm still a pastor to people who hurt.

But there's a weakness there as well.

This is the kind of thing you need to put in your personal journal. Perhaps she was correct, but that's the way I write.

In everything I've written so far in this book, I've tried to be as open as I know how. Part of that purpose is to urge *you* to do the same.

- What specific lack or inadequacies do you feel?
- What can you do to make those needs your strengths?
- What gifts do you have? (All of us have talents.)
- What are the weak sides of those gifts?
- What weaknesses do you have that you can turn around and accept as your special abilities?

As I examine my talents as a writer, I'm also convinced they come out of my weaknesses.

For the past decade, I've learned to value my uniqueness and to lovingly accept the parts of myself that I once ignored or disliked. That's part of my journey toward wholeness.

This chapter began two true-but-negative examples. Those individuals handled their deprivation or emotional hardships badly. Or, I could say their behavior isn't socially acceptable to most of us.

Were they more needy than I was? I don't know, and I don't want to compare. But I do want to point out that they could have turned their weaknesses and deficiencies into their giftedness and strengths.

It's not easy, but you can learn to do that. Your change begins when you recognize and accept your emotional poverty and want to change. It begins with accepting your lack of perfection at being a flawed human being.

Here's one additional lesson I learned, and it's helped me convert my need into my strength: *If I give to others what I wish to receive from them, I am blessed or edified* (or choose your own adjective) *by my actions.* Something mystical and powerful transpires over a period of time.

As I give what I want, I also receive.

Here's one example. In 2007, our house burned down. Alan, our beloved son-in-law, died of a heart attack when he tried to escape from his bedroom.

We lost everything we owned.

I asked nothing from anyone, but the word of our tragedy spread. Within two days the gifts began to pour in—clothing, books, money, and furniture. Jan Coates, a writer and speaker, contacted my friend Stan Cottrell and told him to take me to buy a new computer and printer and sent him a generous check. Her single instruction was, "Don't let Cec go cheap on you."

Steve Laube, formerly my editor and now a literary agent, mailed me nine boxes of books on various topics. Brandy Brow wanted to buy Shirley and me a nice Bible, so she asked us which translations we preferred.

I could go on and on about the gifts. I've kept a cardboard box filled with cards and letters. Many of those kind individuals I've never met, but most of them were people whose lives I had touched in some way.

Some had received scholarships; others spoke of my words of encouragement in their times of need. A few thanked me for mentoring them.

In about a year we moved into a rebuilt house with new furniture. It was a larger house on the same lot, and we had no outstanding bills—largely because of the compassion of others.

I had given, and now others gave to me.

I used my weakness as strength, and in the end, I received the love and affirmation I needed.

I'll say it stronger. In the Bible you can read the Golden Rule. Jesus said, "Do to others whatever you would like them to do to you."[7]

That's how your weaknesses become your strengths. Whatever you want or need, give it to others.

- I USE MY GIFTS TO HELP OTHERS. I ALSO GIVE TO OTHERS WHAT I WANT TO RECEIVE. -

---

[7] Matthew 7:12a

10 · WAITING FOR INSPIRATION

A few weeks ago I was ready to shut down my computer because I planned to work in my flower garden. Just then, an idea flashed for a chapter in this book. Instead of rushing outside, I turned to my keyboard, opened a new document, and began to type.

The words gushed from paragraph to paragraph. I paused a few times to rethink ideas, but within an hour I had completed a full draft of a major article. I could polish it later. In the meantime, I felt calm and peaceful, even though I wouldn't say God inspired me. And it wasn't that powerful, unconscious experience that I would call "writing in the flow."[8]

I believe in divine inspiration, but I don't know how to describe it. In the New Testament, a Greek word that appears only in 2 Timothy 3:16 is usually translated *inspiration (theopneustos),* but it means "God breathed."

I can't say I've ever been divinely inspired. If I have, I certainly don't want to take any credit away from God for working through me. At the same time, I don't want to claim "God gave this to me" so readers blame God for awkward sentences or weak concepts.

Part of my disclaimer is that whenever anyone shows me a manuscript and uses those words, I'm prepared to read dreadful writing, often with misspelled words and unfailingly with grammatical errors. If God does inspire anything I write, I want to hear it as a response from readers who grow from the effect my words have on them.

Let them tell me.

---

[8] See more on this in Chapter 11, "Getting Lost in the Flow."

Think of inspiration as a powerful compulsion to write something that's accompanied by an inner sense of how to write it. Everything seems to flow easily and after you've composed your chapter you say, "It almost wrote itself."

It's wonderful and uplifting. By contrast, when words don't flow well, you probably long for those exciting moments when your fingers can't seem to move quickly enough.

And that's where you have the problem: You can't depend on good feelings; you can't presume on or command inspiration. If you wait for those special moments, you may spend more time waiting than writing.

Think of inspiration as a gift that God *occasionally* (perhaps rarely) sends your way. You don't have any supreme spiritual awareness or sense of being under divine control. In those powerful, pleasurable moments, your full concentration remains on the words that flow through your head and into your fingertips and on to the screen.

I welcome any special ability or intervening experience I receive, but I don't depend on some outside force.

Consequently, to write only when you're inspired devalues the craft and defies your need to learn and improve. If you're committed to excellence in writing, you accept responsibility to do everything you can for your own self-improvement.

Too many writers keep their computers turned off for long periods of time. That's certainly their choice. But some of them say, "I plan to write. I'm waiting to get inspired."

If they're really waiting, they often sit for long periods without any action. I've had experiences like that. Or they shrug and excuse themselves from working with statements such as, "I'll get back to it when I feel inspired."

This may sound like a minor issue, but I'm not just quibbling over a few words. I consider it more serious.

It implies trusting something other than your innate ability. It ignores the need for training. It diminishes the work effort and commitment and prevents you from getting trained and going through the tedium of a dozen drafts of a chapter. It also implies that, to be inspired, you only have to sit, wait, and the divine force flows through you.

Maybe. But not likely.

Something troubles me even more than I've already written. If you depend on that cosmic force zooming into your consciousness, isn't it a subtle message that you're not good enough to do the work yourself? No matter how hard you work, you can't write anything acceptable by yourself, so you're forced to depend on something vaguely known as *inspiration.*

I want all the help I can get, but I'd also like to be clear about my position. I am a serious Christian, and prayer is an important aspect of my life. I pray daily for God to *help me* become a better writer.

As I wrote the above, I thought of a story about a group of professional fishermen who had fished all night and caught nothing. The next morning they gave up and were ready to go home and sleep.

Just then a man, obviously not a fisherman, came up to them and said, "Go back out. There are fish out there, just waiting for you."

Can you imagine how resentful the fishermen might become? A landlubber telling professional fishermen how to do their jobs?

But it's a true story. The lead fisherman was named Peter, who said to the man named Jesus, "We worked hard all last night and didn't catch a thing. But if you say so, I'll let the nets down again." And this time their nets were so full of fish they began to tear![9]

Jesus could have worked a miracle right there by saying, "Okay, wait a minute, and I'll drive the fish into your nets."

But he didn't. Instead he told them to go back out where they had been, put down their nets, and they'd be rewarded.

Miracles don't always seem to work that way. God doesn't usually do for you what you can do for yourself.

Because I work, I receive money to pay my living expenses. I studied in college and graduate schools to gain information, become

---

[9] The complete story appears in Luke 5:1-11.

trained, and able to work for a living. Those are my responsibilities.

So why would God or any other wise power be at your side and say, "Put your hands on the keyboard, and I'll do the rest"?

By contrast, back in the typewriter days, I pasted these words on my electric machine: *Professionals get the work done even when they don't feel like it.*

If you work at your craft and write regularly, you develop whatever talent you have. The more you use what you have, the greater your improvement.

**- I WORK HARD AT MY CRAFT.
I DON'T ALWAYS GET INSPIRED,
BUT I FINISH MY WORK. -**

11 ▪ GETTING LOST IN THE FLOW

Occasionally someone writes or talks about being in the flow or moving into the zone. Despite all their explanations (or inability to explain), they imply this is the kind of writing that seems to create itself.

I'd say it another way: It happens when your writing doesn't pass through a conscious mind filter. You bypass obstructions or yells from your inner critic, and your fingers move smoothly, confidently over the keyboard.

I'm far from an expert, but I experience that surge of words now and then—and certainly more often than I did in my early days. When I get lost in the flow, time has no meaning. I'm hardly aware of anything except the thoughts that rush through my brain and end up on the computer screen.

Far from being in some kind of hypnotic state, I'm aware of what I'm writing and highly energized. The words gush into my mind and, as soon as I type them, new ideas present themselves.

And yet after I've finished, I have to go back and read the manuscript. It's as if I became so caught up in the second-to-second typing, I didn't keep track of what I'd written.

I'm usually amazed at the clarity and simplicity of my writing. I'll edit it later, or perhaps I should say twist around a dozen sentences or change the order of a handful of sentences. The most amazing thing to me is that, despite my intense concentration, I'm hardly aware of what came out of the process. I can say only that the writing flows without a lot of evaluation.

It happens. That's the only way I can explain it.

It's not like what some call *automatic writing*—information coming directly from God or some unknown spiritual source. The information comes from within, and it comes out sounding exactly like me. And I like the result.

If I knew how to induce flow or artificially duplicate it, I'd probably try. Yet the rarity of the experience makes it powerful for me. I wish it would happen every day. Now that I've made it sound glamorous (I assume) and like some kind of spiritual steroid, I'll do what I can to explain it.

What too many scribes don't get is that it happens *to prepared writers.* That is, each time it occurs, it seems to have been the result of a serious struggle with a topic, or the words gush out because of my intense uncertainty about how to approach an article. It happens after I've tried repeatedly to get an idea across and what I came up with before doesn't feel right. And worse, I had no idea how to make it better.

Then that magic moment—the outpouring. It gushes out of me as if it's been waiting inside for me to open the door.

Somewhere I read an expert who insists that this happens as a result of the release of endorphins.[10] When released, the endorphins tend to produce feelings of euphoria. I think that's a good explanation.

Following are two examples. First, when my wife and I moved to Kenya, we wanted to learn Luo, the language of the second-largest tribe in the country. There were no textbooks, and we had to learn it from Africans who spoke English.

I had more difficulty than Shirley because she has a better ear than I do. There is a sound that must come from deep inside the throat and on paper it's written *'ng.* I had a terrible time pronouncing it, but I stayed at it. Many times I wondered if I'd ever learn to speak the language.

The language came slowly, and for months, when I listened to the nationals, I translated everything word by word. When I spoke to the Luos, I had to do the same thing.

---

[10] Endorphins are brain chemicals known as neurotransmitters. They transmit electrical signals within the nervous system. Stress and pain are the most common reasons for their release. They act much like opiates (without leading to addiction).

One day we had American visitors, and that meant we had to translate. I spoke in English while my friend and sometimes-tutor, Henry Nyakwana, translated into Luo. I spoke one or two sentences and listened to his translation, then spoke again.

In the middle of my message, something strange happened. Henry translated my words into Luo. I listened intently, and without being aware, I followed up the next sentence in Luo. Without a pause, Henry translated my statement into English. I'm not sure how long we did that, but there was a moment of awareness. I stopped speaking Luo, turned to Henry, stared at him, and he laughed.

"You are now one of us," he said in Luo.

That day was a breakthrough for me. I had become fluent, and the language flowed.

That's how writing surges in those seemingly magical moments. Without any advance sign, it simply happens. My belief is that flow works on the unconscious level when you're most open to yourself and most committed to doing your best.

As a second illustration, I write gift books for Harvest House Publishers. They asked me to write a book based on Ecclesiastes 3:1-8. The passage begins with "For everything there is a season..." and goes on to "...a time to be born and a time to die, a time to plant and a time to harvest..."[11]

Although I had finished my research and tried to get a mental fix on the book, nothing happened. I tried to write one morning, and none of the words felt right, so I deleted every word. I tried it again and sent a page to my agent.

"It reads like a lecture," she said, and I knew she was correct.

I "wasted" at least a full day not being able to figure it out. I tried reading my research again and tried to write an outline, hoping something would stir. Nothing happened.

In desperation I went for an afternoon run—something I rarely do. I was frustrated and a little angry at myself because nothing sounded right. I talked to myself and to God and tried to focus on the

---

[11] Ecclesiastes 3:1a, 2a

book. No matter what I did, nothing changed.

My mind wandered, and I realized I was tired and wanted to go home and shower. "At least I'll feel better," I told myself.

Just then, I thought about the book and words exploded inside my head—that's not accurate, but it's the only way I can explain it. I knew the first sentence. Just that much. As soon as I was inside the house, I hurried to my computer and wrote those words. The second sentence followed, and so did the next one.

Here's how I wrote the first chapter of the book—and I changed perhaps two or three words:

> Today has been a difficult day. I feel discouraged. That's strange, because two days ago I thought how much I enjoyed my life and decided I wouldn't have it any other way.
>
> Maybe that's the problem: *I wouldn't have it any other way.* I wanted my life to remain forever on that delightful, calm level—to stay the way it is when I feel happy, and life goes smoothly.
>
> But life just doesn't function like that. "For everything there is a season..." [12]

Both experiences have two similar factors. First, I worked diligently and under stress, especially on the language. Second, when the problem moved out of my conscious mind, the unconscious slipped into the control room. My mind tells my fingers, and I'm hardly aware of what's going on.

An unknown writer said, "The ego falls away; time flies, and every thought and movement coalesces in harmony."

On a side note, I'm an extremely fast typist but not always accurate; however, when I'm in flow, my accuracy improves considerably. It's as if my entire being focuses on writing.

I've had other optimal flow times—not often enough, of course. Later, when I've analyzed the experience, here are a few things I've noticed.

---

[12] *Hope and Comfort for Every Season,* Cecil Murphey (Eugene, OR: Harvest House Publishers, 2010) 5-6.

First, I have *an intense inner clarity.* As I type each sentence, I know it's right, and it leads me to the next one.

Second, as I've already mentioned, *time is not even in my awareness.* I may start writing, and the ringing phone will startle me. That's when I'll become aware that I've written for an hour—a few times it's been almost three.

Third, and the most significant, is the *inner calmness, perhaps serenity.* It's the assurance that everything is as it should be. I don't worry about the grammar or syntax. I just write. And yet when I go back, I want to make few changes.

Fourth, I'm *completely immersed and fully concentrating on what I'm writing.* Only afterward do I sense that it's better than my normal writing level.

Finally, I've learned *not to depend on such experiences.* I don't try to make them take place or manipulate my emotions (I wouldn't know how anyway). In fact, it seems to come when I stop trying to control the pace.

But best of all, the flow comes when I'm ready. That means I've prepared myself with what I want to write and know my material. I tend to go through inner struggles first until that magical kind of release.

That's flow.

**▪ I CAN'T MAKE THE FLOW HAPPEN,
BUT I CAN BE PREPARED TO EMBRACE IT WHEN IT DOES. ▪**

12 · HONORING YOUR VOICE

At a California writers' conference in early 2004, I wanted the conferees to get used to me and my way of speaking. On the second day (after we had spent a total of four hours together), I selected five people to read the opening paragraph from five different books. I had printed the words on hard copy for them to read. Each book was on the same general topic.

"All of them come from books in print," I said, "and one of them is mine." The five readers didn't know which I had written, and I didn't want to read them myself in case my own voice betrayed me.

I had previously talked about needing to learn to write with our own voices and to make the words on the page sound like ourselves. "If you write with your distinctive voice, readers will know who you are. People who know me say that when they read my prose, they can hear me talking casually to them."

Before the five people read the paragraphs, I asked everyone to get out a sheet of paper and number from one to five. "As you listen, if you think it's mine, write yes. Write no if you're not sure or think it's someone else."

After all five had finished, I asked, "Which number did you think is my writing?"

Without exception, every person in the class had selected number three. No one missed it. Even though they hadn't been aware, they had learned to recognize my voice. When someone read a published piece by me, it carried the same sound.

That exercise emphasized that each of us has a distinct tone and manner of speaking or writing. For example, my wife reads a number of devotional books and often knows the authors. If it's a compilation, she covers up the writer's name so she can absorb the message. She also likes to see if she can correctly guess who wrote it.

The other day we were driving, and she mentioned a compilation she was reading. She mentioned our friend Virelle Kidder. "I can always tell her writing," Shirley said, and she spoke about the tenderness and the freshness of the tone.

That's the idea: For excellence in writing, your words on paper need to sound as if you're having a simple, direct conversion with the reader. And it doesn't matter which genre you use or whether it's fiction or nonfiction. Your voice is your voice.

I write mostly nonfiction, but I also have published several novels, as well as a few scholarly volumes such as *Dictionary of Biblical Literacy*. The style and subject matters change, but the voice doesn't. When I ghostwrite books such as *90 Minutes in Heaven*, I try not to sound like myself because I want readers to "hear" Don Piper.

Too many writers, however, have little respect for their own sound. You may feel you have to imitate someone else, become more erudite, or use strong words to give you authority. Resist that. Work at sounding like the best possible version of yourself.

At a conference, I spoke about this topic. Several days after I returned home, my friend, Jeff Adams, sent me the following:

> In the movie *Hook*, a grown-up Peter Pan has forgotten how to fly. The lost boys, led by Ruffio, question whether or not the man before them is really their hero. One little boy isn't so quick to disbelieve. The boy peers into Robin Williams' eyes in search of a glimpse of their former leader. In wonder, the boy exclaims, "Oh, there you are, Peter."
>
> Peter had forgotten who he was.

Readers choose certain authors the same way they select their friends—on the basis of personality—or the sound of the author's words in print. All humans have a circle of people who like them and want to be around them. You also have those who don't like you, avoid you, or can't relate to you. That's the same as your readership.

If you're like the average person, you want to have more friends—and as a writer, that refers primarily to buyers and readers of your writing.

Your readers aren't attracted nearly as much to characters or plots as they are to the personality—the voice—the style of the writing. If they like your voice, they'll be open to embrace your characters or your principles. Although readers may be initially attracted because of the subject, unless you provide a personality to the material, many won't continue to the end of the article or book.

Too many writers don't resonate with readers because there's nothing distinctive about them. That is, they hide themselves from readers. They use the right words, good material, and no one faults their thinking.

That's the problem: They're bland. Perhaps boring.

One writer friend sent me the first three chapters of a proposed book. I told him, "It's as good as thirty other books; it's not better than thirty other books."

I also said, "I have no idea who you are after reading this material. Part of your role is to show yourself to me—you do that through your writing voice." I know the man fairly well and like him immensely, but I said, "The man I like and the man on the page don't know each other."

I want to be clear: No matter how truthful you are or how self-revealing, everyone won't like the *you* they meet on the page. Some people don't read my material and don't like anything I write.

Occasionally several people will rave about a bestseller and on their recommendation I buy a copy. I read a couple of chapters and wish there had been a refund policy. Different tastes.

You can't expect everyone to like you or to want to be listed as your friend. Neither should you expect everyone who picks up your book or article to feel an instant kinship with you.

You'll collect friends and fans as you write more—and especially when you write from who you are and sound like your true self.

No matter how much some editors or other writers may not like your writing, you'll attract those who will. You'll draw people into your writing circle the same way you do in your friendship circle.

Much of that depends, of course, on your delivery. One person can tell you a story about something that happened and you listen attentively to every syllable; another may tell the same story and you fidget, want to help move it along, or stop listening.

Writing is much the same. Learn the craft and the techniques, but just as important, write with your distinctive voice—that is, capture yourself on the page. How you communicate is as important as what you write.

Your voice comes out of your experience, your view of the world, and especially your self-understanding. The more aware you are of yourself, the better you communicate your attitude about life or any specific topic. To find your true internal tone isn't a one-for-all experience. It's ongoing. The more you write (and especially the more you publish) the more you grasp your voice.

For example, I'm a right-to-the-point person. I try to be as straightforward as possible. Others may not like me or my direct tone, but if they read me, they'll know certain things about me, such as my candor.

That frankness (some might call it bluntness) didn't come with my first article. It's been an ongoing process. As I've become more open and self-appreciative, my words on paper become stronger and truer to reflect who I am.

Here's what I call the ultimate purpose: To find, honor, and use your voice, you have to be ruthlessly honest with yourself. Many writers fail because they hide part of their true selves. They either don't accept all of who they are, or they feel ashamed to write from within.

I can say it differently: Writing with your true voice is to write with honesty, vulnerability, and with risk. Especially notice the word *risk*. It demands your venturing outside the conventional pathways to say, "Here is who I am, this is what I believe, and I'd like you to appreciate me and my words."

Don't lie by using safe words. Don't be dishonest by conforming to what others claim as their standards, and certainly don't perform so that others applaud your cleverness and syntax.

Writing with your true voice—authentically—doesn't mean writing subjectively (although there are times you may do so). Writing with your voice means you trust yourself and your material enough to write with your unique vocabulary, your style, and your outlook on life.

No one can teach you to write with your true voice. We instructors can only provide the atmosphere or setting that honors the process and encourages you to strive to hear your inner voice.

Please remember this: The true voice is the heart of good writing. It's more than techniques or the ability to write in more than one genre. It's the ability to accept your voice as valuable and to use it.

**▪ THE MORE I KNOW WHO I AM
AND LIKE WHO I AM,
THE TRUER MY WRITING VOICE AND
THE MORE FAITHFULLY I HONOR THAT VOICE. ▪**

13 • EMBRACING YOUR VOICE

Think of your writing voice as *your* natural way of producing words. You have a texture, a sound, and a rhythm that's unique to you, and it's your power source.

And, as I wrote previously, it's not a once-in-a-lifetime experience. That's both the joy and the frustration. You're aggravated because, as you grow, you face the reality of your petty attitudes and judgmental feelings.

Readers and editors may not always point them out, even though they sense the voice isn't quite consistent. On paper you may exhibit your true self more than you're aware.

I want to tell you the first time I became aware of that fact. Shortly after I started to write, I read a book by a woman on the topic of divorce. I was a pastor, seeking resources to help such hurting people. A large publisher issued her book, so I assumed it was good.

I read it and never recommended it to a single person. Perhaps four years later I met an editor from a different publishing house, and we became friends. I mentioned that particular book and, before I had a chance to comment, he said, "I haven't read it, but I've turned down everything she has sent to us. She's an angry person."

Those weren't his exact words, but he knew her as a person; I knew her as a writer. Both of us knew the same person. And neither of us liked her very much.

We both agreed that the woman was talented, and I felt she wrote well, but it was the underlying anger that crept through the prose. That's the best way I know how to explain the effect of voice.

I know a writer whom I like very much, but I don't like most of his writing. He's published many books, and they've sold well. Perhaps it's because I know him, but when I read his fiction, I feel his characters are stilted. He writes for the Christian market and, unkind as this may sound, my friend's writing is boringly orthodox. Nothing new, nothing controversial, and certainly nothing exciting, even though there's a lot of action in his novels.

He plays it safe. And that's all right. I don't condemn him or want to speak harshly against him. I believe he does the best he can, and I don't think he'll ever burst through the self-barriers.

To say this in a different way: If you write something that's generated from your inner self, you're connected with the material. Readers can lose themselves in your prose. One writer says that it "turns readers from spectators into participants."

"I want to discover my natural voice," someone says. "Tell me how."

The common advice is to say writers need to begin with what they know. Maybe.

I think it's better to say, "Write about what stirs your emotions."

Don't all of us feel through the language of emotions? If you combine that with good writing techniques, you have a good start.

"Teach me how to discover my true voice" is an easy request.

But the answer isn't simple.

Here's my response: I don't know how. Even if I did, the emphatic word is *discover.* If I show you, you're not discerning and seeking. You're merely following my direction, and I may be wrong.

You have to find your own way; however, I can offer you a few suggestions. But first I want to explain why I can't or won't try to teach you.

I taught sixth grade for two years. I have a natural, backhand slant—it's just there. Before the end of the first week of school, my sixth-graders had begun to copy my penmanship.

To combat that, I worked quite hard for a couple of weeks to make my cursive writing look as much like the standard penmanship the children were supposed to follow. As I expected, their penmanship improved.

When I began to mentor scribes, the same thing happened. One woman changed every sentence to read the way I edited it, even though I said, "Say this in your own style." Her manuscript read like an imitation of my voice—an inferior imitation—as it usually is when it's not the natural voice.

More recently I've offered suggestions and urged students to use their own words. That approach has seemed to work well. I suggest what they might do and let them revise the material, and telling them they can disregard everything I've mentioned. That approach takes longer for them to complete an acceptable piece, but they also learn in the process.

What I tell them is simple: Be as natural as possible—but be correct. People need to be able to *hear* you—the authentic you.

Finding your voice is like being on a sacred quest. Respect your search because your voice is a gift from God that's unique to you.

As you learn to trust yourself and your personality, you learn to recognize your voice and style. You write sentences and you smile. "This sounds like me," you say.

Your role isn't to negate, abhor, or abuse your writing, but to recognize, value, nurture, and honor it.

Here's another way of looking at the topic. Your voice has an inner dimension and an outer dimension. The outer is your style, your way of writing, telling a story, or explaining a solution. It reflects the way you think and the way you see the world around you.

The inner dimension is the messenger. You take in information or grasp truth, but you first digest it and make it part of yourself. You have to listen to the inner part of yourself—your authentic sounds. The "information" becomes part of your value system. Or, as some say, "You have to own it."

Once you integrate the new into the old, you can deliver the message you have to offer. It's always an ongoing search. You push away once-useful techniques and knowledge because you replace them with more accurate, up-to-the-present method and data.

If you really want to find your voice, your goal is to journey toward inner wholeness—which is what life is about anyway. It involves self-acceptance and genuine self-respect.

This may be redundant, but I want to stress that finding and honoring your voice involves self-acceptance and self-love. When you've learned to honor your own voice, you also appreciate authors who are different from you, and respect the unique range of voices.

So here are questions to help you get started.

- *What do I want to write?* Don't say, "What's popular?" or, "What do agents want to see?" What stirs your passion? If nothing else, you'll begin to figure out if you want to focus on fiction or nonfiction.

- *What issues or deep concerns do I have?* They're the kind of things you think about a great deal. Justice, love, tranquility, freedom, or war—those are all possible answers.

- *What are the unresolved issues of my life?* For example, early in my writing career, I sold many articles about human relationships. I get along fairly well with people, but I wanted more of something in my life, and I didn't know how to define more. My writing was part of my search to figure out and resolve issues in my life. And that has happened many times.

I encourage you not to settle for surface, obvious answers.

As I pondered my own questions, friendship is a topic about which I was passionate. What I sought (but wasn't aware of it) was for one or two intimate relationships I could trust and individuals to whom I could open myself without wondering if they would betray my confidence or laugh at me afterward.

In that search, I began to envision my writing as walking down the street with an intimate friend on either side. I put my arms on their shoulders as we walked and I said, "I have things I want to share with you."

- *Is my writing honest?* That may sound insulting, but I read so much dishonest writing. By that, I mean statements that proclaim great truths and wouldn't cause anyone to question their meaning. But is that what the scribes think, or how they think they're supposed to believe?

But suppose you look at your own work in progress. Ask yourself, "Do I truly feel that way?"

To ask such questions opens you to possible solutions or directions you hadn't previously considered. You don't have to think like the people among whom you work, recreate, or worship. You're responsible to be honest with yourself. If you're honest with yourself, your writing will reflect that.

I'll answer the question about honesty for myself. I was a member of a particular Christian denomination for eleven years. They were mostly good years, and I wasn't unhappy. But I read books—many books—including those authored by insightful individuals with different theological perspectives. I didn't ask if they were right or wrong, because I wanted to understand what they were saying and what they believed. I wanted to widen my theological horizons.

By the tenth year, I realized I had changed in a number of ways. I didn't turn from God or join a cult, but the theological differences between the people with whom I worked and my own understanding changed.

We lived in Kenya during that final year, and I devoted most of my time inviting pastors and church leaders for two or three days of teaching. I set up a course of study with notes for them to take home.

As I changed, I asked myself: "Should I impose my new understanding on them?"

Some of my new understandings opposed the theological positions of the group that sponsored me.

I decided I couldn't. I had come to the country with a group of people who were solidly committed to certain theological principles, and I had moved toward a different set. To teach my insights—even though I was convinced they were correct—would have been liberating for me but troublesome for the Africans and other missionaries.

Instead, after six years in Africa, we returned to the United States and I went to seminary. I chose a seminary that emphasized the theological perspective I had accepted.

That's not about writing—at least not directly—but it's part of who I am. Being honest with myself was to admit that I might be correct (and I still think so many years later), but it wasn't right to impose my newfound thinking on the Africans or my coworkers.

Four years after our return to my own country, I began to write and to sell. Because I had honorably shifted from one theological group to a different one, I realized two things.

First, I was able to be honest about what I believed. Second, I was able to understand those with whom I disagreed. Why not? I had once been among one such a group and still respected them.

That was a special step in finding and embracing my voice.

For me it comes down to this statement: The more comfortable you are being who you have become, the easier it is to write with your voice.

■ MY VOICE EXPRESSES WHO I AM. IT WAITS FOR ME TO DISCOVER AND EMBRACE IT. ■

14 ▪ FINDING YOUR VOICE THROUGH OTHERS

The first time Shirley and I saw the Barbra Streisand-Robert Redford film *The Way We Were* we raved about the powerful story and the believable characters. Even though the story begins during World War II, we identified with the timeless theme of human emotions in action.

One of my favorite things after seeing a film is to discuss not only the plot but to recognize parts of myself in the characters. Gender isn't a factor; I focus on the motivation and attitude.

As we talked, Shirley became quite vocal about her emotional connection, but after several sentences, I realized something: Even though both of us empathized, we weren't talking about the same person.

She identified with Hubbell, the Robert Redford character, who played life safe. He was nice, easygoing, and didn't want to stir up troubles or problems.

I laughed because I understand Kati, the Streisand character. She was the maverick, the outspoken one, the stand-up-for-what-you-believe individual who would never let things slide along.

We had a delightful time discussing the film over dinner. Neither the Redford nor Streisand characters were totally who we were. Yet each provided a candid snapshot of one facet of our personalities.

Shirley prefers the calmer, safer lifestyle, which is about the opposite of me. Perhaps that's why we do so well together. I used to say I was constantly looking for a new mountain to climb and Shirley's voice implied, "This is a good place to pause and enjoy the scenery."

Either position is valid, but our preferences are different.

That's true with your writing voice. Certain writers speak to you through their prose, whether it's fiction or nonfiction. You may have a favorite writer or book at one time and change later. That may be one way to look at your growth.

Here's how it worked with me. When I was in my teens, I read *Les Miserables* and loved it—even though I wasn't sure I understood, and I skimmed large portions.

Most of all, I understood Javert, the police inspector. He knew rules; life for him was right or wrong, and there was never anything else. I realized years later that Javert represented the family background from which I came. It's the way my parents operated—on the black-or-white system.

I *understood* Javert, but I didn't resonate with him. I felt sorry for him when, near the end of the book, he doesn't know how to be grateful to Valjean, the escaped convict who saved his life. Javert knew law and passionately pursed wrongdoers, but he couldn't handle grace, and he couldn't forgive.

I also identified with the protagonist, Jean Valjean, for many reasons. I didn't see any parallel in our lives, but I admired his strength of character (as much as his physical strength) and saw him as a man of integrity who fought injustice and loved the orphan girl, Cosette.

I've since read the book three more times. The last time, perhaps four years ago, I closed the book and felt deep sadness for Javert, who had nowhere to turn when confronted by an act of undeserved human kindness, so he drowned himself in the Seine River. In the previous readings, I hadn't felt that way.

What does that book tell me about myself and my growth? Here's one thing I figured out. Over the years I've felt both pity and compassion for the hurting and the destitute. I've realized how much I value kindness, especially the self-sacrificial attitude of a man like Valjean. He was hunted by an overly zealous, unrelenting man of laws and rules. But Valjean was able to push away his anger, pain, and desire for revenge, and do the right thing.

If it's true that we're like the characters in the books we read, the obvious implication is that connecting with the author or the writing helps you to form your writing voice.

Instead of merely enjoying a novel, what would it be if you paused to ask:

- *Which character mirrors me?*
- *What can I learn about myself?*
- *Which characters do I dislike the most? Which ones anger me?*

I saw the splendid 1940s film *Wuthering Heights*, with Laurence Olivier. Critics praised it as an enduring love story.

On film, perhaps.

Then I read the book, and I detested Heathcliffe.

He was unscrupulous; he took advantage of others' weaknesses; he was self-centered and ruthless. Perhaps I had such a strong reaction because he reminded me of some of my baser motives and attitudes.

In sharing these books and films, I assume you may be someone who "becomes" the characters you read or watch. If you pay attention to your emotional response, you can gain insights about yourself.

Let's transfer that to writing. Decide on one or two writers with whom you identify. When you read, whether fiction or nonfiction, those authors speak words that penetrate your heart. They nudge you toward growth and improvement. They stir you intellectually. They motivate you to act.

I also suggest that you find writers who make you say, "I wish I could write that well." Let their writings become part of your lessons on improving as a writer.

A little-known writer named E.B. Kenyon spoke to me when I was in my early twenties. The best word I can use today about his writing is *simplistic.* And in this case, I don't mean that as derogatory. He wrote in short, terse sentences at a time when most writers rarely inserted a period until they had used a minimum of two commas and a hundred words.

I was a new convert to Christianity. His fourth-grade sentence structure spoke to me, and he taught me basics of the Christian faith. I understood him in ways I hadn't grasped from the erudite teachers.

I mention Kenyon because, without consciously attempting to emulate him, he helped me become the writer I am now. Long before it became vogue, I wrote short sentences and brief paragraphs. Some editors and readers said my writing was choppy—and by the standards of the late 1970s and 1980s, they were correct. But I was discovering my voice and experimenting. I liked Kenyon's style, stayed with it, and probably irritated editors.

I suggest you sample the writing of as many authors as possible. Close the book on those you don't like but avidly read those who make you think or feel or say, "I wonder if I could ever be that good."

What grips you about a specific writer? What do you remember from the style or the language? Sometimes those influences are minor, and they may also be negative.

Even the negatives can be educational. During my first two years of college, we received an adult Sunday school take-home paper. It seemed as if a woman named Betty Swinford wrote in almost every issue. I liked the stories, but her clichés wore me out, and I became sensitive to such hackneyed expressions. The example I remember most was that whenever people had a crisis, someone made "gallons of coffee."

Gallons? Two people or even six people? I stopped reading her, but she impacted me.

Isn't that obvious? I remember her writing after half a century.

Although I sell largely nonfiction, I'm an avid fiction reader. I discovered one novelist by paying ten cents for a used book in 1988. For the next twenty years I bought and read everything he wrote. About that time he became extremely popular and his books hit the top spots on every best-seller list. They still do. He experimented and turned out books that helped me immensely.

In one book, he has no back story. We learn about the characters and situations only when they speak about themselves as the story unfolds. He does it well, and that's a tribute to his talent and his technique.

Many times I'd pause and say, "I wish I could describe a scene like that." Or I'd think, *That's powerful dialog.*

In my opinion (and apparently many reviewers on Amazon agree with me), his last two books don't have the quality and the warmth of his previous ones.

Even so, I learned from him. He wrote with heart. I felt the emotions his characters displayed. Many times I copied whole paragraphs because I liked the way he phrased sentences. When he described anything from nature to a kitchen to a man's physique, I could visualize it.

Another writer who helped was the late Henri Nouwen. I never considered him an outstanding writer, but his introspective attitude and spiritual insight spoke to me. I yearned for the level of inwardness I read in his books. I wanted the depth he seemed to display.

Today I'm grateful for all the writers from Victor Hugo to Henri Nouwen. They helped me discover my voice.

▪ I FIND MY VOICE THROUGH UNDERSTANDING OTHERS. ▪

15 · GROWING YOUR VOICE

figured out something else about myself through my reading. I like thrillers, and my wife prefers books that have a high level of romance. That doesn't even need explanation.

More recently, I gained insight on the kind of adventure books I chose. I rarely read novels about nuclear destruction of the world or a programmed computer that, if unchecked, would destroy the economy of developed nations. The ending is obvious from the beginning.

I'm pulled toward the more intimate thrillers. The accused man who is probably innocent. The woman who's being stalked and threatened and doesn't know who or why. Someone has embezzled millions of dollars from the firm, and the evidence points to the honest protagonist.

I like the type of action-suspense where there is a killer or a serial murderer—what I call the "contained" thriller. I can make sense of a hunt for a serial rapist in New York or Atlanta. They're large cities, but my mind can navigate through the streets.

I also like defined characters. I want to picture the males and females, and I like it when the heroes aren't six-foot-six but more average like the rest of us, and the same with the females. Sure, I want her pretty, but she doesn't need to look as if she should be on the cover of *Vogue.*

What does that say about me? *Intimacy* is the first word that comes to mind. The more I get into the heads and hearts of the major characters, the more satisfying it is to me. And it's easier for me to identify with average people.

I regularly have lunch with a friend who likes what he calls "the bigger-picture setup" in books. He wants action, action, action. He likes the techno-thrillers where readers learn more about nuclear submarines and plans to destroy Israel than about the protagonist or antagonist.

Do I need to tell you that my friend, whom I like very much, isn't particularly warm and emotional? He has a first-class brain and rarely trusts his gut instincts. Does his preference now make more sense?

■ ■ ■

Previously, I asked you which characters in books and movies hold up a mirror to your personality. That's a good start, but our world is filled with mirrors for us to see ourselves. *If we pay attention.*

Years ago one psychologist insisted that the automobile was the most common sex symbol in our modern society. According to him, people choose a car (unconsciously) that says, "Don't look at me, but look at my car because that's the real me." Or perhaps the message is, "That's who I wish I were."

The message is the same with the adoration of sports teams and fanatical fanfare.

The colors we wear mirror our personality. I'm aware of this by the clothes I choose each morning. I like wearing bright colors, but some days I want more shadow than sunlight so I pick muted shades. Even if I'm not aware of my mood, my clothes tell on me.

The list goes on and on and says that each selection you make is a reflection or mirror of who you are.

Perhaps what I've written above seems patently obvious, but the question that arises is "So what?"

Let's say you recognize some of those mirrors. What do you do about them? Or perhaps the question is, "Does what I write reflect the truths of my life?"

Here's the answer: The more consistent your reflection is with who you are, the stronger your voice.

I recently reread *Oliver Twist*, which I've never particularly liked, but it made me aware of one of the issues of Charles Dickens. Ever notice how often he speaks of impoverished, orphaned, or crippled children? Tiny Tim, Oliver, David Copperfield, or Pip. Doesn't that hold up a mirror to Dickens? He also tackled social issues, and that's another reason I admire the man.

Earlier I mentioned *Les Miserables*. Hugo also wrote *The Hunchback of Notre Dame*. I don't know how anyone can read those two books without grasping issues of social injustice—among other things—including compassion for the weak or scorned.

Someone told me that most of us have only a limited number of themes that loop through our lives. I've often heard that it's four or five. Here's how I see themes at work in my own life.

I've probably written in as many different genres as anyone and I've ghosted or collaborated on many books. As I've thought about the books I've written that have impacted me the most, it's easy to pick up the theme: I'm passionate about underdog stories. Ben Carson, for whom I wrote *Gifted Hands* and *Think Big*, is the best example.

In fifth grade, Ben was at the bottom of his class until he learned to read and by the time he graduated from high school, he won a full scholarship to Yale. He later became a world-renowned pediatric neurosurgeon. That's my kind of man; that's my motif.

Here's another message that comes out of my books. In 2008, I began to write a series of gift books for Harvest House on the general topic of caregiving. In some ways they're the easiest books I've written, but they're also the most difficult.

Caregiving implies emotion, transparency, and openness to hurting readers. When I focus on one of those topics, my emotions come to the surface.

Occasionally readers will say, "You understand. You know how it feels to hurt."

If I do, it's because I've paid attention, especially to the mirrors in my reading. As I read those who stand a step or two above me on the ladder, I become better. My writing voice improves because their words and theme mentor me and help me improve my voice. They took risks with their themes and that helps me to take risks.

If you are free to expose yourself, and I identify with your risk-taking, you win. I also win because I become a better writer.

• I LEARN FROM OTHER WRITERS. I GROW MY VOICE BY PAYING ATTENTION TO THE WRITERS I LIKE TO READ. •

16 ▪ LEARNING FROM YOUR DAYDREAMS

He's a meek accountant who daydreams about exciting, heroic events that take him out of his boring life. That's a one-sentence summary of James Thurber's classic short story "The Secret Life of Walter Mitty."

Mitty drives his wife into town to shop. On the way, he daydreams that he's a pilot flying through the worst storm in twenty years. Afterward, he's a famous surgeon, a wartime general, and a murderer on trial for his life.

In the final daydream, Mitty stands alone, facing a firing squad, and refuses a blindfold. Instead he smokes in a nonchalant pose as a way to say death means nothing to him.

I liked the story because it told me what I had assumed: All of us daydream; few of us talk about it.

Not only do you have such reveries, but you'd probably be ashamed or embarrassed to talk about them. Keeping the contents to yourself is fine, but pay attention to them. You can become aware that daydreams are your unconscious mind being able to imagine anything it chooses. Those awake-dreams can help you discover your writing voice.

Perhaps, even more, they can guide you in acknowledging and examining your passions in life.

I daydream. Often. A lot. I go to sleep at night with a concocted storyline inside my head. I let it play out until I fall asleep (which, my wife insists, is less than two minutes). I'm always the hero, although sometimes I'm the innocent who is crushed by adversity. Even when I'm victimized, I'm of stellar character and noble deeds.

They may not say who I am, but they certainly tell me who I want to become.

Think about your daydreams. Sometimes your unaware imaginations—another way to describe daydreams—focus on your anxieties or worries. What does that say to you about yourself?

Long ago I realized that when I faced an unpleasant situation, I focused on it a great deal. I envisioned the worst possible outcome of every crisis, even with minor problems. That's no longer true because I've learned more about my daytime dramas and listened to what they told me.

Daydreams connect with what we now call *self-talk.*

Self-talk doesn't revolve around what happens to you, but what you say to yourself internally. Your inner chatter, the experts insist, determines your thoughts, feelings, and actions. They say your self-talk determines the majority of your emotional choices. That's because the words you use to describe what is happening to you, and how you feel about external events, trigger the emotions of happiness or unhappiness you experience.

They'll also tell you that if you control that inner dialog, you can control every part of your life. I'm not willing to go that far, and my position is slightly different. Listen to yourself. What messages do you hear repeatedly in your imaginings?

Above I mentioned Walter Mitty, which was my first serious awareness of awake-dreams and their power. The second came years ago when I read biographies of star athletes at about the same time positive self-talk became popular.[13]

The athletes admitted that they quietly visualize what they want to accomplish. A professional bowler, for example, might visualize himself approaching the foul line, letting the ball down smoothly with a powerful follow-through motion, and watching his ball hit solidly between the headpin and the third pin for a clean strike. He sees the score sheet with twelve Xs for a perfect game.

That's the method supposedly used by top coaches and star athletes. Their mantra seems to be, "If you can see it, you can achieve it." That's a bit extreme for me, but I think self-talk is an important

---

[13] All of us talk to ourselves and we refer to that as *inner dialog.* Positive self-talk gurus cite it as one of the most powerful influences on attitude and personality.

aspect of monitoring and directing our free-floating thoughts.

As I've already said, some experts say that you and I and everyone else have a handful of themes or issues in our lives—and those issues continually repeat themselves.

So what?

You have a choice. You can allow your negative themes, fears, or worries to rule your life, or you can intervene and change the storyline.

For example, I stopped envisioning the worst that could happen in a troublesome situation. Instead, I focused on the most positive outcomes. When the real events came, they were rarely as bad as I had once imagined, and they weren't nearly as wonderful as I had hoped.

I can report two positive results. First, I know myself better by monitoring my daydreams. Second, my anxiety level has decreased.

I urge you to pay attention. You can figure out the deeper meanings about what you say to yourself. But even more, if you analyze them, you'll gain a bigger picture of who you truly are and how you feel when no one is watching.

But first you need to be aware of those mind-wandering experiences. The following questions may help you think more readily about your daytime adventures.

- When do you find your mind wandering?
- Do certain situations or activities trigger your daydreams?
- Are your daydreams generally negative? generally positive?
- What role do you play in each of your daydreams? Are you the protagonist? the victim? the innocent? the guilty?

In recent years scientists have demonstrated that daydreaming is a fundamental feature of the human mind. Some now call this our default mode of thought. They argue that daydreaming is crucial for creativity because the unconscious thought process allows the brain to make new associations and connections. (I like that explanation.)

Instead of focusing on your immediate surroundings, such as listening to a lecture that bores you, your mind floats to pleasant thoughts. You pull yourself out of the numbing experience as your mind soars into new, creative heights. You might plot a novel or get an idea for a how-to book.

You're able to imagine things that don't exist and explore possibilities for action. If your mind didn't take those creative vacations, you'd be focused on everything you do, including the things you do by rote.

Monitoring your daydreaming can be a powerful method for you to understand yourself and your desires.

How do you use your daytime dramas as writers? My simplest answer is that you open the door to explore ideas. It's an unconscious way of asking, "What if?"

Suppose you're not sure what to do next in your writing. Let your mind soar and play freely. That's what I do. I monitor myself, but I don't interfere. Afterward I think about where my thoughts went. I also ask myself one question: "What did my soaring thoughts communicate about me?"

Here's one example. One time the Power Ball Lottery was above three-hundred-million dollars. I was with a group of friends and someone brought up the lottery. Several of them said what they'd do if they won all that money.

I've never purchased a lottery ticket, but I thought about what I'd do if I were the solitary winner. To my surprise, I couldn't think of anything more I'd like to buy. I might want a new car, but I liked my three-year-old Honda Hybrid. I didn't need or want a new house. Clothes? Perhaps I might buy two or three new neckties.

If I didn't need the money, what would I do with it? My mind flowed on, and I focused on the various ways I could give away the money. Sometimes it was anonymously, other times through setting up foundations.

And yes, I had heady thoughts of banquets in my honor for giving millions for research for AIDS or Alzheimer's—all with me acting appropriately humble.

That daydreaming was immensely helpful to me. My unconscious mind proved something to me. Many times I'd said aloud that getting wealthy wasn't significant. On other occasions, events prompted me to think about receiving or inheriting large sums of money. Each time, my thoughts flashed on the best ways to give it away. The greater the amount, the more tedious it became to be wise in parting with the funds.

I hesitated writing that because I don't want to come across as some self-denying, totally altruistic person. My wife would say I do embody those qualities, but they're not all I am.

I've also monitored those mindless trips that worried me or caused anxieties. Here's an example. I had collaborated on a book, finished it, and sent it to the publishing house. The editor emailed that she had read it, would get back with me, and "We can talk about the editorial changes."

Editorial changes? What does that mean? My mind took off and anxieties dominated my thoughts. I imagined everything from tossing away the entire manuscript and starting over, to being fired from the project, to needing to edit every sentence.

When she did get back to me, she really meant that they were now doing editing online through Adobe and wanted to explain their new system.

I could have said to myself, "All that worry was for nothing." Instead, the anxiety helped me realize how much I cared about the project—and doing a good job. And it reminded me that I continue to struggle with insecurity.

■ ■ ■

Listen to yourself.

Listen to your inner chatter.

If you constantly devalue yourself or call yourself derogatory names, that says you need to start affirming yourself with positive self-assertion statements.

You can grow in awareness by paying attention. Some people are aware; but for others, the daydreams and thoughts become clatter, like an out-of-focus movie that runs in the background. By noticing your daydreams, you can learn to see your long-held (maybe even long-buried) goals.

Whatever your daydreams are about, teach yourself to see the goal or purpose. How does it affect you? What do they tell you about yourself?

▪ MY DAYDREAMS TEACH ME WHAT'S IMPORTANT TO ME. MY FIRST TASK IS TO PAY ATTENTION TO THEM. ▪

17 · DO YOU WANT TO SHATTER WRITER'S BLOCK?

'**ve** rarely met a writer who didn't speak about being unable to write at some point. In the years I've been in this profession, I've read an innumerable number of articles on how to break through the blockage, and many instruction books contain at least one chapter on the topic.

We call it *writer's block,* and it's usually defined as a temporary or chronic inability to type words that appear on the screen. It's nothing new, and one man who produced a total of six books in eighteen years said (boastfully perhaps), "Until you've been stuck and unable to write for months at a time, you're not a real writer."

I disagree with him, but I assume he's talking about his own experience.

Most of the books, articles, and blogs on writing view writer's block (WB) as an obstacle in the path or writing. Your role is to push the blockage off the road, jump over it, destroy it, or go around it. It becomes the enemy you must defeat, because it prevents your being productive.

That's the popular approach. And it works for many authors. I'll list some of the methods they suggest.

(Although I've changed the wording slightly, the following material came from my friend Don Otis, who is a writer and a publicist.)

- *Interruptions.* Limit them because they interfere with your creative concentration.
- *Time.* Discover your best time to work. Is it mornings? Evenings?

- *Folders.* Put resource material for a particular writing project in an accessible manila folder or have a special document file on your computer.
- *Exercise.* You regain energy and often receive clearer insight.
- *Deadlines.* They keep the pressure on you. (If you don't have a due date, create one for yourself.)
- *Timing.* Start important writing projects early so you aren't forced to rush to finish.
- *Think Time.* Give yourself space and permission to ponder your project.
- *Pray.* Wail at the Wailing Wall for wisdom and direction.
- *Location.* Change where you're working. Go to Starbucks, a library, or sit in your car with a laptop. Go into the country or to a retreat center.

■ ■ ■

For many writers, any of these methods enable them to overwhelm or defeat the dreaded enemy that blocks their progress.

And it makes sense. Suppose you're talking to someone about the wonderful book you read three days ago.

"Who's the author?" your friend asks.

"Uh, right now I can't think of the name." You're embarrassed, but you know that if you divert your thinking, the name will return. You move on to something else. A couple minutes later you say, "That author's name. Now I remember."

The bullet points above help many, many confused authors to defeat the enemy that blocks their mind and energies.

But there's another way. Instead of seeing WB as an enemy or alien force, why not turn it around? Why not ask yourself, "What can I learn from WB?"

I'll go further: *WB is your friend.*

Focus on that thought and ask yourself:

- "What if WB is a symptom and not a cause?"
- "What if WB comes from some wise, inner part of myself that wants to help me?"

- "What if battling WB is really fighting my deeper, inner self??

I have moments when I'm stuck, but not often. I tell my students, "I once had writer's block, and it was the most miserable *hour* of my life." Although that's meant as a joke, WB isn't a humorous condition. For some people, especially the chronic sufferers, WB is like a disease for which there's no permanent medication. They go into temporary remission, only to relapse repeatedly.

Because my book focuses on you, the inner writer, I won't offer eight exercises for you to use to overcome the terrible disease. What I will offer is my insight into affirming and accepting WB.

There's no guarantee, but if you lovingly accept WB, you might end up being healed.

Let's start with this: WB happens when you can't push ahead. "Something's wrong," you say. The problem gets worse. The immediate tendency is to panic, fight, argue, prod, or even curse the demonic spirit that stops you.

Let's first think about the issue of being unable to figure it out. That's why it's a blockage. Here's the question to ask: **What** *is going on inside me that stops me from writing?*

I ask that question with an emphasis on *what* and wait for an answer. When WB happens to me, I'm convinced something is going on inside my subterranean region. The unconscious stumbles and seems unable to get the connect message to the conscious part of the brain.

Suppose the unconscious shouts, but the sensory part feels only the effects. If this is true with you, it's not some passive, quiet problem, but one that yells, "Stop! Stop!" You hear the cry even though you have no awareness of the cause.

As an analogy, I don't know much about automobiles, but if I'm driving along and the engine dies, my question is, "What went wrong?"

I don't ask, "Why is my car not cooperating with me?" I'll check to make sure I have enough gas, but beyond that perfunctory observation, I don't know what to do. I assume that the vehicle has been trying to give me the message for days, perhaps weeks, but I wasn't getting it because I don't know the language of the combustion engine.

The car finally dies on me. Now I *must* pay attention.

That's how I see WB at work in my own life. If this feels right to you, I urge you to listen to your subconscious. Open yourself to solutions, even though you may be stalled a long time.

First, *consider WB as a powerful force to help you regulate the creative process.* It's an insistent voice that lets you know something is amiss—it may not tell you specifically, but you know your creative drive isn't functioning quite right.

Here's how I say it: Your unconscious self vetoes the commitment of your conscious ego. It stomps its foot to say, "I don't care what your head demands; I'm not cooperating."

Second, *think of your ability as a gift from God*—even if you don't feel you're a gifted writer. One successful author once told me, "You don't own those abilities, and they function as long as you treat them with respect and appreciation. When you try to control your talent, it fails."

I like that statement, which also tells me that because it's a given ability, there is no limit to what you and I can do as long as we function with integrity. Haven't you heard people speak of a particularly able person as one who wasted his talent?

Third, *consider the blockage as one that comes from within, not an outer force that works against you.*

Consequently, suppose you said to the holding-back part of yourself, "Thank you for resisting. Thank you for stopping me from moving in the wrong direction. Enable me to listen and to learn."

■ ■ ■

The single, most troublesome thing about WB of which I'm aware is that it comes when we write against our values. While writing this book, I spoke with my friend Nancy McGuirk. She talked to the board of her organization about her next writing project. They told her what they felt she ought to write, and she agreed to do what they recommended.

"But it wasn't my passion," she said. "It was a good topic, and I could do it, but I've had to push myself through each chapter."

That's an example of what I mean. You try to write something you don't believe or attempt to become enthusiastic over a topic that holds little interest. Like Nancy, you might be able to accomplish the project, but you can't give it your total, emotional involvement.

Years ago I used to hear beginning writers, especially women, say, "I'm going to write a romance. They're easy." I can't think of one such individual who sold one. The words "They're easy" gave them away. They jumped onto a genre because they assumed they could think of a clever storyline, complete it quickly, sell it, earn a lot of money, and move on to the next book.

They didn't lean in that direction because of excitement about the genre; they tried to write because they thought publishers wanted romance novels. Further, they mistakenly thought "anybody can write a romance," and they would have no problem writing or selling it.

Every genre has specific "givens" and, especially in the early days, romance was one of the strictest. But those tyros went ahead— and few of them finished.

My friend Gary said, "It was hard work, I had to learn too much, and I didn't have that great an interest anyway." He stopped with Chapter 11.

One of my friends signed a contract for a book because an editor convinced him he could do it. Later, after he returned the advance, he told me, "I was writing something I did not feel, did not believe, did not care about, and I avoided writing what I did care about because I didn't think it would sell."

He feared that the publisher wouldn't offer him any future contracts, but he knew it was the right thing for him to do. (He did write for that publishing house again.)

Fourth, *what if you said, "This is a chance to learn more about myself. This is a chance to find out what's truly important to me"?* If you sincerely did that, you might be amazed at where your writing takes you.

Fifth, here is the secret—or at least it's what works for me. I ask most of the questions in this chapter. *Then I listen.* Sometimes waiting for an answer is an intense experience.

I listen. Often I don't hear for days, but I still listen.

Today I had lunch with an especially gifted writer named Ginger. She had something she wanted to write, although her agent told her it wouldn't sell.

"Should I write it anyway?" she asked a group of us. "Should I forget about it?"

Here's the answer I gave her: "You know what to do. You may not know that you know, but deep inside, you already have the answer. If you don't know or can't face the answer, wait. Wait until you hear."

As I re-read the above, I could envision a reader's hand waving in the air. "What happens if I don't get an answer?"

Ginger didn't ask that question but others have.

"Keep waiting," is my response. "Determine not to write until you're assured of what you're supposed to do."

I continue to listen until I feel certain, and sometimes it's accompanied by excitement. Most of the time I already have a hint—a sense—that I've driven down the wrong road or that I refuse to face the topic on which I need to focus.

Most of the time I don't know exactly what's amiss, but I've learned to hang on until I do.

I may divert myself with something else such as reading or watching TV. I wait even if it seems I've focused on something else. I allow the unconscious part of my mind to work.

For me—my personal strategy—I usually opt for a run. At the start of my hitting the streets, I ask the question and, within a minute or two, my mind wanders or turns on any subject such as the weather, what I plan to do with the rest of the day, or what to plant in that section of my garden that gets no sunlight.

I run, often up to six miles. Something about the monotonous pounding of my feet lulls me into a listening mode.

Then the answer comes.

Usually it comes in a way that's so reassuring I'm ready to go to work immediately. Sometimes the answer seeps into my conscious mind, especially if it's something I've strongly resisted. Other times, it's like a brain shock. The solution is often so obvious I can hardly believe I didn't know. The incoming message may say, "You don't want to do this. You don't care enough about the topic to throw your heart into such a project."

I listen. When I run and I "hear" the answer, regardless of how the answer comes—as a blast, a whisper, or a single sentence—I know when it's the right one. The words carry an authoritative ring.

I've learned to trust that internal voice. And so far, it's proven faithful.

For example, years ago a publisher asked me to write six devotional books and gave me the topics. I liked all six and did them quite rapidly. The publisher wanted another four, which would have been fine except I didn't like two of the topics. One of them would be called *Devotions for Insomniacs.*

I rarely had a problem with sleep, and it wasn't a topic I cared much about exploring. I wrote all of them except the one on sleep problems. I couldn't generate excitement about insomnia. I could go to my local library for research material. I could easily access the information I needed, but I couldn't work up enough enthusiasm.

I asked my editor for permission to give the project to Phil Barnhart, a published writer I knew well. Insomnia was an ongoing problem for Phil, and my editor agreed to let him do it. Phil did a good job. Perhaps I could have forced myself through the process, but I didn't want to try.

The best way I know to avoid or overcome WB is to be kind and compassionate toward yourself. Instead of demanding, "Get this done!" or treating yourself harshly, "You're lazy! You're stupid!" you can ask softer, kinder questions, such as, "If you'll tell me what's stopping you, I won't push you to do it if we can't resolve the problem."

One time I had a book offer—and I'm a fast writer—but the publisher wanted the book in less than a month. My initial response was to say to myself, "I'll have to work long hours for the next month, but I can do it."

Just then a new thought came to me: *Do I really want to work that hard? Do I want to neglect everything else in my life so I can complete this project?*

As soon as I asked myself those questions, I knew it wasn't a project for me. I turned it down.

The only time anyone has argued with me about my approach was one writer who said, "What about self-discipline? Can't you be disciplined enough that you'll be able to push yourself to do it?"

She missed the point of discipline, so I said, "I'm not a slave. I love to create, but I have to do it with passion. I can't force passion; however, if I'm enthusiastic, there is no need to push myself."

She thought of strict self-regimentation—and for some people that may work. It's like following a totalitarian leader. You don't question or argue. You just do it.

Some may write under such conditions.

I don't, and I won't.

I respect myself too much and honor my talent too highly to force myself to write against my interests or values.

One final thing: Writing takes on a rhythmic pattern. Lows are as inevitable as the highs. You can learn to reinterpret the experience. Instead of feeling guilty for not being productive, you can say, "I need to stop and be clear about my next move. I'm going to declare a holiday until I'm clear about what I'm supposed to write."

My good writing develops inside my head long before it becomes words on my computer screen.

**- WHEN I'M BLOCKED,
I LISTEN QUIETLY AND COMPASSIONATELY.
MY DEEP, INNER VOICE WANTS TO TELL ME SOMETHING—
SOMETHING I NEED TO KNOW. -**

18 · IT'S HARD...AND GETTING HARDER

For a long time I thought it was an individual issue. Later I decided it was something only writers endured. From there I discovered that artists, singers, and other professionals also suffer. Maybe it's something common to people in most areas of work.

Here's my dilemma. The more I write and the more honest I become, the worse my writing *feels*. This is an emotional issue, not a logical problem.

In early 2011, I sent a completed nonfiction manuscript to Summerside/Guideposts to fulfill my contract with them. I felt it was the worst book I had ever written.

Who wants to read this garbage? This is awful. The publisher will cancel the contract. Those were a few of my tormenting thoughts.

The book idea had come to me months earlier after I spoke with the V.P. of Product Development, Jason Rovenstine. I sent him two sample chapters. He liked them.

So did I.

Then.

As I continued to write, however, I became increasingly distressed. The doubts knocked softly, but I kept typing. The critical voice became more volatile with each page I wrote. I persevered.

I discovered that others suffer from a similar malady. An article about the once-famous singer and movie star, Deanna Durbin, said she quit singing because of her intimidating insecurity. She often vomited after a performance. I read something similar about Jean Arthur, one of the great screen personalities of Hollywood's golden era. A friend said the same thing about Barbra Streisand's inhibitions as the reason she stopped performing regularly.

That's the dilemma. The feelings become so powerful I struggle to fight against their insistent racket.

At the same time, I sense that if I weren't growing and exposing my deeper self, my "palace guards" wouldn't be on alert. That's my word for the protective side of my personality—the part that doesn't want me to be hurt.

Three experiences have helped me in my struggles to accept my palace guards. The first time, years ago, I realized that when I wrote *my* books it seemed to get harder each time.

I mentioned it to Steve Laube (now a literary agent but who was then my editor). "I'm glad to hear that," he said. "I wondered how deeply you felt about what you wrote." He mentioned a highly respected writer, "who fights that all the time."

I remembered Steve's words, but I must have pushed the issue from my mind, because for the next five or six years, I seemed untroubled.

Then the doubts hit me—worse than ever. I spoke with another editor, Steven Lawson, and told him about the internal conflict. "All I can tell you is that your writing gets better and better."

He was trying to comfort me and encourage me—and his words did—but nothing improved emotionally.

The third experience was after I sent my manuscript to Summerside Press. About two weeks later, I received an email from Jason:

I've read through Chapter 7 and love it! It's real and honest, and it offers hope. It's just like my friend Cec.

His words encouraged me but they didn't solve my dilemma. They did make me more open to myself. They enforced my commitment to move deeper into myself, no matter how painful. And the pain was sometimes excruciating.

Three times outsiders encouraged me; they didn't seem bothered about my struggle. Two of them considered it a positive experience. If the two editors were correct, and if Jason especially liked what he read, what did those voices mean?

They meant the others spoke objectively while I fought

subjectively with my inner demons.

Or maybe they're not demons.

What if those tormenting words are for your good?

What if the voices are there to help you?

What if they want to protect you?

That final question opened a wide door of understanding. What if the words came from a wiser, deeper, inner part of myself? What if those are protective devices—ways to stop me from doing something foolish or awkward?

That's when I labeled it "the cry of the palace guards." Those soldiers stand their ground and remain on the watch for enemies and threats. Their single duty is to protect me from embarrassment or humiliation. They don't want me to be too transparent or too honest.

Instead of seeing them as fierce, angry palace guards, I changed my way of thinking. No longer did I see them only as arbitrary, angry police officers, but I viewed them as my loyal, faithful, and loving friends. They didn't want me to get hurt or wouldn't stand for the possibility that others might take advantage of my transparency.

That was the word that explained things to me: transparency.

The more I revealed about myself, the more I moved out of the protected shelter. "People might not like me if they know who I really am," I wailed to my protective, compassionate guards.

The answer came back to me in the form of an aphorism I've already shared once in this book but repeat it here because it's so critical to my own development (and perhaps your own thinking):

**I would rather be disliked for who I am
than to be admired for who I'm not.**

Whenever my fears begin to sneak inside my head, I repeat those words aloud. I have to decide if I want to censor myself, or if I'm willing to become vulnerable—even more vulnerable.

I've chosen transparency, and it's an ongoing option. I want to be honest, so that who I am permeates each page as I write.

Here are my two major reasons for doing that.

First, *it's one more step toward wholeness and self-acceptance.* It means I push away thoughts that inhibit me from being honest with God and with myself.

Second, *if I'm transparent, I offer readers like you the opportunity and encouragement to open yourself and allow your palace guards to back up a few feet.*

Each time I write, I strive to be as transparently honest as I can, and that's when the doubts arise. I haven't found a cure, but here's how I understand it.

The deeper I go into myself, the more internal pain I endure. The trouble comes from a natural, self-caring element inside me (my palace guards) that wants to protect me from criticism, foolishness, or mawkish writing.

Sometimes I pause and reflect on struggles of the past. I remind my guarding friends, "You've saved me from many bad writing projects by correcting my mistakes or showing me better ways to slant an article. Thank you."

"Why wouldn't I love that part of myself?" I ask. "You're there to protect me from myself and I love you for doing that."

I send out a monthly newsletter and, several months ago, in the midst of my internal struggle over writing this book, my brief essay focused on this struggle.

The response overwhelmed me. To my amazement, my readers understood. Several shared their experiences or told me about people they knew. Here are two of them.

The first is from a writer named Phil Cohen:

Writer's rut. I can't stand the smell of my own writing. Afraid I'm going to rehash what I've already written. Afraid people are getting tired of reading my stuff.

Then I got a newsletter from Cec Murphey, a best-selling author who has written more than 110 books. It appears he struggles with the same thing.

I think most artists struggle with this. We read about great and talented musicians who take their lives. The relentless chatter of their inner critic finally drives them off the edge.

Back when I was playing lead guitar in the church band I got to where I couldn't stand my own sounds. The church people said I was doing fine, and I should keep playing. I was determined to play with authenticity, from inside the notes, and not imitate another musician or hide behind the music. The sound of "me" was repulsive to me. But I played through the pain, and it ministered to others. Eventually, I came to like that part of myself.

God has given me a gift for writing about my journey to inner spiritual growth. Many of you identify with my wrestlings because you wrestle with the same things. I'll continue using my gift to serve you in love, even when it's painful for me.

Here's a response from my friend Phil Leftwich: "I have found that all creative people feel this way." He recalled one NYC Broadway theater lighting designer who said "Every time I start a new project, I internally say, 'This is the one that I'm going to blow it on. This is the time that everyone will find out that I'm a hack.'"

Here's the rest of Phil Leftwich's email:

You are right too in that an artist's latest works are often their greatest. A Christian music publisher told me once, "You should always be getting better at songwriting, because the more experiences you have, the better your songwriting will be. The best song you will ever write should be one that you write on your deathbed." Kind of morbid, but I believe it's true.

With many of the songs I've written recently, I've felt that same vulnerability you've described. Open. Too honest. Too human. Not going to be popular.

But in a world where there are millions of songs and books, I believe it's the ones that include those vulnerable elements that will capture the attention of the seeker. More and more, I think people will be seeking honest art. Sincere art. Vulnerable art.

Just wanted to send some encouraging reflections your way. Your insights are valued.

I sighed when I read those emails. I'm not the only one, and it felt good even to feel miserable in the company of my friends.

> ▪ I AM COMMITTED TO MOVE DEEPER INTO MYSELF, NO MATTER HOW PAINFUL. ▪

19 · "BECAUSE I WAS AFRAID"

This morning I thought of an old story about three men who were to manage a business while their boss was gone for several months. They were to carry on the business until his return. When the man came back months later, two of the men had done remarkably well with the company. In their respective areas, both had doubled their employer's money.

Doubled! They had been amazingly industrious, and the boss praised them both.

He turned to the third man, the one who had received the smallest amount of the business capital. That employee had done nothing with the money. He hadn't lost any, but he hadn't invested in the stock market, opened a savings account, or put the funds into CDs. If there was any good in what he did it was that he kept the money safely hidden so no one would steal it.

When he gave his report, the angry boss castigated him.

I tell this story because of the response of the third man. "I was afraid I would lose your money," was his lame excuse. Perhaps he was too afraid of doing something wrong, so he did nothing. His fear kept him traumatized.

I've just modernized a story Jesus told, often called the parable of the talents.[14]

Although that's not the point of the story, think about the man's justification. "I was afraid," he said.

That's the honest statement of many, even if they don't say the words.

---

[14] See Matthew 25:14-30

I understand that third man, because I was afraid to write this book. For years, I fought undertaking this project.

Someone passed on comments about fear in business writing, but it's just as true in every genre.

George Orwell, author of *Animal Farm* and *1984*, wrote, "The reason business writing is horrible is that people are afraid. Afraid to say what they mean, because they might be criticized for it. Afraid to be misunderstood, to be accused of saying what they didn't mean, because they might be criticized for it."

That statement says it well. And I was afraid for all those reasons.

Last week I had lunch with three other writers. We spoke about what was going on in our writing lives. I admitted my fears and doubts.

Nancy McGuirk laughed. "You've written more than a hundred books, and you're afraid?"

"Yes."

To most people who know me, my emotional attitude probably seems silly and only a pathetic excuse. But it's true.

I'd already written, co-written, or ghostwritten 122 books, but I was still afraid. I'd lost count of my published articles, but they must number close to a thousand, yet fear still clutched at me.

Since 1984, I've supported myself as a writer. Comparing myself to others in this profession, I have a prodigious output. That's all true, but I was still afraid.

I didn't recognize the problem as fear...at least I didn't at first. It started seven years ago when an editor at Writer's Digest Books suggested I write a book on the craft.

I resisted the invitation to submit a proposal. I told myself I was too busy ghosting for others (at the time I had contracts for three books), and I was too engaged in my preparation and teaching. (In those days I taught in at least fifteen conferences each year).

That was what I said, but I knew busyness wasn't the reason. I wasn't ready to write a book about how to improve the writing craft. I finally asked if I could send a book proposal about the person of the writer and received a thumbs-up.

I did (finally) write a proposal. The editor told me it was too straightforward and wasn't off-beat enough. (*Kooky* was the word she used.) She wanted something more in line with Anne Lamott. I don't write like her, so I was secretly relieved.

That wasn't the end of it. About a year later a woman asked if I would co-write a book with her, and I declined. My honest answer was that I felt I still didn't know enough about the craft. And that's true—I'm still learning. At the same time, fear nibbled at me.

For nearly four years, my assistant, Twila Belk, pushed me whenever she could sneak in an attack, and I balked each time. My agent, Deidre Knight, believed in the original proposal of this book and said at the time, "I wish all my clients had a copy."

At a writing conference in Florida, for two years in a row, an editor urged me to write a book to help authors learn their trade.

My answer wasn't, "I'm afraid," but again I said, "I don't know enough yet about the craft." That part is true: I'm still trying to improve and feel I have things to learn.

One day I faced the real struggle. I'm quite self-revealing in my writing, but I wasn't ready to be nakedly transparent in front of my peers. Other readers maybe, but this would be a book for other professionals—whom I knew, liked, and respected. I didn't want them to laugh at me. Or to rephrase George Bernard Shaw and scoff, "Those who can, write books; those who cannot, write how-to books."

Who am I to tell other writers how to get inside themselves?

■ ■ ■

What brought about my freedom to write?

Earlier this year, I came back to the idea of a book. I couldn't get away from the idea. I kept telling myself I didn't have time, that it wasn't something I cared about doing, and I'd get around to it eventually. I thought it would be a nice, safe book to write after I decided to retire. Because I have no idea when that will be, it was a safe self-promise.

I'm a fast, self-disciplined writer. I tend to get an idea, research it, work it through so I know where I want to go, and it's finished within four months max.

Because the idea wouldn't vanish, I kept asking myself one question: "What's going on that I don't want to write that book?"

No matter how many times I asked myself that question and listened for an answer, no solution came.

One morning, just before 5:00, I did my morning run through the dark streets of my neighborhood. I asked myself the question when I started, pushed it from my mind, and focused on other things.

Three-quarters of a mile from home the answer came.

I knew.

"I'm afraid," I said aloud.

Saying the words wasn't enough, so I asked myself the next question: "Of what am I afraid?"

As I pondered, I realized that such a book would force me to lay myself on the line. Readers would identify my true self, who I truly am, and I wasn't sure I wanted them to recognize me. If I completed the book, I would lay myself out there for public scrutiny and readers could gaze with undisguised disgust.

"And he wasted how much time in writing this tripe?"

"Why didn't someone tell that nice old man to hold his index finger on the delete key?"

"He must have been desperate for money to write this junk."

Inside my head I heard the smirks and dismissive comments. Someone would read a page or two, smirk, and say, "Sure, but who doesn't know all that?"

But the worst—the absolute worst fear—was (and still is): "What do I have to say that will help other writers?"

In my struggles, I also faced another reality, and that's part of the fear. Some people might not like what I write; others might not like my style; but worse, they simply might not like *me.*

One of the joys of being a ghostwriter, which is where I've made most of my income, is that it's safe. I hid behind other people for whom I've written several bestsellers. My own books were mostly in the inspirational category with moderate sales. I wrote two critically acclaimed scholarly books—critically acclaimed but poorly sold.

In Chapter 17 I focused on writer's block. Perhaps fear is another name or at least one of the symptoms. But for me, it wasn't blockage as much as it was an unwillingness to write.

I hadn't hesitated to put myself on the line with other things I've written. "What makes this different?"

As soon as I said those words to myself, I knew the answer.

I'm going to say this several ways, and all of them were sentences that flashed through my mind. They're irrational, and I want to make that clear. Fear doesn't recognize logic. Fear is a primitive emotion that doesn't know how to listen to reason. Here they are:

- I'll be defenseless. This is about a craft, an art.

- Writers will laugh at me. "He taught others, but he can't write about the craft."

- People will know I'm a fraud. I create a lot of sentences, and they flow easily, so I've fooled myself into thinking I'm fairly good at what I do.

- No one wants to buy a stupid book about going inward. The editor at Writer's Digest told you as much. Writers buy books about the craft, the how-to approach, not stupid introspective garbage.

- You're not a therapist, so don't try to act like one.

- What if my book isn't helpful or encouraging? What if my book discourages would-be authors?

- What if I've fooled myself into thinking it's better than it is?

- I get tired of those tyro writers who tell me how good they are. I usually assume it's a protective device as if to say, "If I tell you I'm good, you can't argue with me." It also tells me that they're in denial—unwilling to learn how bad they are. *Is that who I am?*

Fear keeps us running (or paralyzes us) and reminds us that we have to take risks to succeed, and we may not be ready to jump into literary empty pace. I felt like an alien, who landed in an unfriendly universe.

But I also knew that fear can be helpful. Facing that reality became my turnaround moment. Fear means I'm stepping into virgin territory. I'm writing things I haven't articulated before.

Here's what I told one friend:

> When Murphey does his best writing, he's both excited and apprehensive. The excitement works, because he knows he'll learn new things about the craft and perhaps gain new insights about himself. But that's also the source of his fear. It's easier and safer to keep producing products in the areas where he succeeded in the past.

One morning, after battling inner terror and deep anxiety, I was still on the brink of indecision. I promised myself I would decide before the day was over. I was trying to find a satisfying way to say no to myself.

That afternoon I received an email from a man in the UK. He thanked me for something I wrote to him nearly three years earlier. He had been afraid to send out his manuscripts, but I read several of his articles and thought they were good, told him so, and encouraged him to send them to magazines.

"Your words finally crushed my resistance."

At the bottom was the email I had sent to him three years earlier. Accepting my fear is where I discover my most creative moments. For me, vulnerability often brings panic and always some apprehension.

Yet I also know that the more I open myself to myself, the more creative, passionate, and interesting my writing becomes. It's also hardest for me to write during those times.

Trapped by my own words.

■ ■ ■

I finally wrote the proposal for this book. Immediately after the title page, I put one paragraph in a box and labeled it *Concept.*

> Murphey contends that too many write on the surface. They don't go deeply into themselves and so they don't feel frightened. Consequently, they write on safer topics and the fear goes away. Then they assume they don't have a problem or they've overcome it. They've taken the safe route and haven't "overcome" the fear; they've covered (denied) it. We can fight the fear, deny its existence, or accept that we're afraid.

Other fears and anxieties crept in as I began the writing process. I know myself well enough that I assumed I wouldn't find an easy solution. In fact, I realized that I probably wouldn't lose the fear. Even when I'd almost finished this book, trepidation continued to stalk me.

Sometimes my inner critic only sneers.

In writing other books, and some of them have been difficult, I've struggled with fear. So it's not a new emotion.

For instance, I wrote a book called *When a Man You Love Was Abused*, about male sexual abuse. As a survivor of childhood sexual and physical abuse, my purpose was to reach out to help other men and especially to encourage the females who love the emotionally wounded males in their lives.

As I wrote that book, not only did fear snatch at me, but some days the pain returned in such force, I stopped writing for an hour or even a whole day.

I kept on with that book because, strange as it may seem, I was aware of the fear, but it was something I *had* to write, as if I had no will of my own. I had to tell others about those of us who had been molested as children.

I felt I was on a sacred mission—standing up for something in which I believed. But that was different. I wrote for a *cause*.

This book is different from anything I've previously published because it's about the inner writer, and the concept seemed flat and insipid.

I might have gotten beyond writing this except my agent and I had lunch one day. She reminded me of the long-buried book proposal. "It's time for you to get it out and produce a book on writing."

I was able to admit my dread to Deidre.

"Too many writers won't acknowledge their fear, and when they eventually come to the place where they realize they're afraid, they freeze." She paused before she added, "You need to write it for those still behind you on the pathway."

No matter which direction I turned, everything screamed, "Write!"

This chapter may be worthless to you, but my purpose is to say that fear is a common enemy. I'm not the only person with such dread. The trepidation hits most, perhaps all, serious writers at some point. We become apprehensive or panic stricken.

Once I acknowledged my fear, faced the "signs" God had placed in my path, and especially my own words in a long-ago written email, I knew I had to respond. That fear wouldn't disappear. Worse, it would probably intensify and spread to other parts of my work.

I had to take the risk.

I had to give myself to this task.

And so I did.

▪ I FEEL AFRAID WHEN I BARE MY SOUL. I RUN THE RISK THAT OTHERS WILL DESPISE ME, RIDICULE ME, OR IGNORE ME. BUT THAT'S WHO I AM. THAT'S ALL I HAVE TO OFFER. ▪

20 ▪ DO I HAVE TO WRITE *THAT?*

I had finished a keynote address at the Write to Publish Conference in Wheaton, Illinois. A woman with tears in her eyes rushed up to see me. Half-coherently, she told me the sad story of her background and a rather sordid lifestyle. As I listened, I wondered how that connected with my message.

She stared at me before she dropped her head and lowered her voice. "Do I have to write about that?"

It took several seconds before I made the connection. I had spoken about being open and truthful in our writing.

"Do I have to write that?" she asked. "I don't want to do it."

"Then you have the answer," I said. "Don't write about it."

She smiled through tear-stained eyes.

"You don't have to write anything you don't want to write...but is it something you *need* to write?"

"I can't get this out of my system." Her lips trembled and tears slowly flowed down her cheeks. "It's just that it torments me."

"I spoke about getting in touch with your inner self and being honest with who you are. I stressed the need to probe inside, to find who you are, and to write from within. Is that what you understood?"

She nodded.

"Do you have any idea what's going on inside you that makes you feel tormented about this?"

"No."

"Really? Think about it some more." I sensed she wasn't being honest with herself.

"I don't think I'll have any inner peace until I write it."

Our conversation continued, and I urged her to consider the difference between needing to write about her experiences and forgiving herself for her past.

That shocked her, and she made me repeat my words.

I said them again because I wanted her to realize that writing is an opportunity to move into the deeper parts of ourselves. "That doesn't mean you have to write everything you understand. The writing process becomes a tool for deeper soul penetration."

She sat silently for several moments, and then she smiled. "I get it. I know where to dig, but I don't have to expose my findings."

Then I smiled.

Some of my most powerful insights have come when I've been in the midst of ghostwriting for celebrities. It's not the writing itself that makes the difference but the inner openness. I focus on them and try to sense their issues and feel their pain.

My first ghostwriting project was for a famous singer who told me he hadn't had a healthy relationship with his father. Consequently, he constantly sought older men to induct them into the role. He hired several old men, and none of them ever fulfilled his expectations. Probably none of them could.

As I worked on the manuscript, I realized how much I yearned for a healthy relationship with my father. In the process I felt the rejection again from my own dad. I didn't have to write my story, but in the process of writing for the singer, I touched my deeper emotions.

Once you gain insight about yourself, you become stronger and emotionally healthier. Your writing is different, but the principle is the same. If you're open to yourself, you gain insight and realize the implications of how it affects your thinking and your behavior.

Once you integrate the new into your life, that's the time to ask yourself whether you need to write about it. Sometimes that's exactly the path to take.

But not always.

Here's something typical of what I hear regularly. My late friend Rich Stanford had a heart attack when he was about fifty years old. The experience transformed his life. He told me it forced him to face his mortality and to value the gift of life. He changed his lifestyle, began to exercise regularly, and to eat differently.

About three months later he called me. "I'm going to write a book about my experiences with a heart attack."

I didn't try to argue him out of it, but I was sure he wouldn't be able to sell such a book. I did ask one question: "How would your book be different from hundreds of other serious-sickness-to-recovery stories?"

He went into a long justification, and I understood. He had survived a death sentence, and he couldn't stop thinking about it. A natural reaction, especially for a writer. He never wrote the book.

I've heard from many others who have gone through horrendous experiences. Afterward they feel they *must* write about it. Perhaps six times a month I receive emails from those who have survived traumatic experiences. "Everyone says I need to write a book" is a typical sentence. In the next paragraph they ask for my help.

That's a natural response. When something powerful happens, and especially after an unexpected, life-transforming experience, it becomes the major topic of conversation. They sometimes speak of life before the distress and afterward, as if they have lived twice.

If they're writers, they probably live by the concept that any experience becomes raw material for writing. I agree with that. But it doesn't mean they have to produce a book or an article. It may mean they need to live with the experience for a time. Or they may want to hold the incident and relate it at a more appropriate time.

Timing. Readiness. Both are factors.

Here's what I mean in my own life. I was sexually and physically molested as a child and coped by "forgetting" it (that's a form of denial). When the memories began to return, I still didn't write about the abuse for several years. I sensed the day would come when I would be able to talk or write about the subject without tearing up.

About ten years later, I wrote articles for two different magazines and felt I had said everything I needed about my abusive childhood. A second decade went by before I published a book on the topic.

During those years, I often thought about my past. I went through the stages of forgiving my perpetrators, and of learning to affirm myself. I needed inner healing from those childhood wounds.

It wasn't until I had great peace about the abuse issue that I was ready to focus on a book. I was past the anxiety as well as the need to blurt out my story to anyone who would listen. I had not only healed sufficiently to discuss it without my emotions crumbling, but I was able to view my childhood with some emotional detachment. That is, the world didn't revolve around me and my experience. I had been victimized, but so had thousands of other boys.

Let's go back to the original question: Do I have to write *that?*

My answer is still the same. No.

But.

The real question is whether you feel compelled to share your pain, recovery, or insight, and you won't have peace until you do. And I also say, "Tell us more than what happened. Tell us what you learned about yourself. And if you didn't learn something that embarrasses or shames you, perhaps you're still not ready to open your heart to the world."

Playwright Arthur Miller once said, "The best work that anyone ever writes is the work that is on the verge of embarrassing him." That says it well for me. If it's easy or simple to write, it probably isn't what I'd call poignant or powerful.

Years ago I wrote a book about prayer and laid out the problems I had in maintaining a serious, devout life. Now, years later, it seems like such a simple thing to do, but it was extremely difficult for me to write—then. It was my first book, and I didn't know how people would respond.

To my amazement, the most common response was readers thanking me for being honest. One woman wrote, "You put in print what I often think but can't say."

That simple sentence infused me with courage. And along with that I was prepared for bigger risk taking.

> ▪ WHEN I WRITE FROM WITHIN,
> I PUT INTO WORDS WHAT OTHERS THINK
> BUT CANNOT SAY. ▪

21 - DISCOVERING YOUR RHYTHM

Most of the professional writers I know can tell me of a time when they were highly energized and finished an article or a story quickly. "It almost wrote itself," they say.

But that's not the usual response. Most of them talk about how hard it is or the difficulty to keep going. Elsewhere in this book I refer to writer's block and my own struggle with fear.

This is different. This is more of what I call *ennui.* It's weariness or tedium.

You have the ideas and know approximately what you want to say. But you can't push yourself to write. You put it off. You promise yourself to do it later that day or in three days.

All of us have different working methods, and I urge you to find whatever works best for you.

Some writers say, "Deadlines amuse me," because they don't meet deadlines or they struggle to make them. Collecting information to enrich a scene or clarify the point of an article becomes an ever-ongoing task. Multiple ideas fly through their heads. They tend not to want to let go of their research (or their polishing or rewriting—whatever they call it).

"I continue to enrich my manuscript," one such person said to me. He called it *enriching;* I labeled it *procrastinating.*

Their well-organized counterparts love to finish a project. They love routine. Editors love such individuals because they meet deadlines. Always. But they may become so consumed with finishing a project by the deadline that they make hasty judgments. Unless they learn to hold back, they turn in unsatisfactory manuscripts.

Some people can work only when they face that dreaded word called *DEADLINE.* They think about writing and perhaps even do a little work inside their heads. But for them, no serious action takes place until they say, "This book is due in five weeks! I can't put it off any longer."

From that moment, they divorce themselves from everything else and get to work. They barely make the due date (with minutes away from midnight) or they write a plaintive email: *Please give me three weeks' extension.* They list twelve reasons, but none of them are valid.

That's who they are. If that's a picture of you, admit it, and accept that as part of your personality.

Live with yourself. You might change a little, but probably not much. The best piece of advice I can offer is to be who you are and live within your preferred way of doing things. You probably went through high school and college with that pattern.

When I was in grad school, most of the students hovered in little groups only nights before finals and stayed awake for thirty-six hours to prepare for tests or write semester papers.

I'm a polar away from that approach. I've always been fairly well organized, but when I was in graduate school (two of them simultaneously), I had to make every half hour count. I did it, but I wouldn't advise anyone to emulate my behavior. One school was on a quarter system and the other was on a semester basis, which was probably the reason I could do both and not have ten final papers due at the same time.

I carried that style with me into my career. When I began to write, I was a pastor of an exciting, growing congregation. I set aside one hour every morning before my secretary arrived. *One hour.* I couldn't sit and stare into space.

During the day I visited as many as seven hospitals in metro Atlanta, and I used the travel time to edit inside my head. When I arrived at my office the next morning, I pecked at that keyboard without pausing until my secretary entered the building.

These examples are to say that you need to find what works for you. Don't try to follow my pattern. You have your own rhythm, and you're happier and more prolific if you follow your natural bent.

Twice I've received emails from a man I've never met. "I keep trying to be like you," he wails. "And I'm not making it."

Of course he isn't. He's not Cec Murphey. Both times I've pleaded with him to be himself and follow his own energy rhythm.

Here's another fact. I'm an early riser. I'm up to run around 4:30 and I'm at my desk anytime after 7:30. By 4:00 in the afternoon, my brain says, "Sign off for today," and I do.

Some professionals aren't energized until 10:00 at night. They do their best work and go to bed about the time I get up.

My wife tended to be the charge-up-at-night person. I tried to adapt to her in our early days, and I absolutely couldn't. She has modified her lifestyle to become a closer match to mine.

When I was in high school, I worked one summer. They asked me to work the night shift after school started. I tried it for two weeks and still couldn't stay awake, so I quit.

I tell people, "You can call me as early as you like, but don't talk to me after 9:00 at night."

. . .

As the wise man in Ecclesiastes says, there is a time for everything. That means there is a time not to write as well as a time to write. That was a difficult lesson for me to learn.

For my first twenty years in publishing, I slavishly followed the advice on the craft gleaned from one of the first books I read: *Write every day. Never miss a single day.*

I felt guilty if I wasn't always productive.

It took me years to realize that (a) I didn't have to write every day; (b) my writing was of better quality if I wrote only five or six days a week; and (c) sometimes I needed gestation periods.

"There is a time to write and a time not to write," Richard Foster wrote. "I've just finished a period of a year and a half now where I felt God told me not to write. He wanted me to learn some things and to be quiet."

Foster's comment helped me. I copied it and kept it pasted on the corner of my PC tower for at least a year. I knew it was advice for me.

By June, I've usually planned most of the following year. As I planned the end of last year, I sensed I needed to pull back, enjoy my life more, and not feel pushed to keep up a hectic schedule.

It wasn't a sabbatical because I faced writing two twice-weekly blogs, a monthly newsletter, and I had page proofs coming up for two books. I had pulled back once before, around 2006, and didn't write anything new for three months. When I returned to work, I was eager and filled with ideas.

From late October of last year through January of this year—a little longer than I had anticipated—I read constantly. Someone gave me a Kindle and I downloaded a number of classics such as *Phantom of the Opera, Sense and Sensibility,* and *The Picture of Dorian Gray.* I read contemporary books, fiction and nonfiction. At one point I floated through three books a week.

Writing, like any other phase of your life, needs to take on a rhythmic pattern. You'll have the low times as well as those days when your fingers can't type fast enough to stay up with your mind.

My hiatus periods have been wonderful. It's like the adage about filling up the well. That's what I do. I also think about books that I want to write. But it's more. The doing-nothing time gives me a chance to refocus. I ask myself if I want to continue producing the kind of books I've been doing. What stirs my passion now that I didn't think about a year earlier?

Here's how this came about. More than thirty years ago, I began to run on an indoor track at a health spa. Unconsciously, as I made the eight laps to a mile, I increased my speed. In those days I wanted to build up endurance and not speed, so when I became aware of my increased clip, I couldn't seem to just slow down. The only way I could change the momentum was to stop, walk a lap, and start to run again.

That lesson came back to me in 1997. For ten years I had written nothing but books for other people—ghostwriting. Two or three had my name on the cover, but most of them didn't, and lack of recognition was no problem for me.

For years, my wife had nudged me to write my own things, but I insisted I had nothing to say and that anything I wanted to write, someone else had already done it—and done it better.

One day, I heard my own words say, "If I have to ghostwrite

another book, I'll quit." Those words surprised me, but I knew they came from deep inside me. The only way I knew how to rethink and refocus was to stop writing completely.

That was my first time to walk a lap. Three months later, I had refocused. That's when I wrote my own book and a publisher bought it. The book didn't sell well, but that was all right, because I had accomplished what I wanted to do.

I had told friends I wouldn't ghostwrite again, but after five months, I was ready to do it again—however, more selectively, as well as collaborating on fewer books.

I had to find myself. And for me, it meant pulling totally away from my profession for a short period.

Here's what I'd like you to get from this chapter: By pulling away temporarily, you can refocus or reassess your writing. You don't have to be productive every day. For some people that's not a problem, but for compulsives (like me), it takes a major decision not to be productive and not to feel guilty.

I also remind myself that the best part of my writing takes place inside my head. It's the thinking, discarding, rethinking, and absorbing more of life that leads to my best writing. That takes place long before words appear on a page.

I remind you to be whoever you are and to follow your own natural bent. Don't try to emulate me or anyone else.

> **• I WANT TO BE THE BEST ME I CAN.
> SO I FOLLOW MY NATURAL RHYTHM,
> AND DON'T TRY TO IMITATE ANYONE ELSE. •**

22 · SEEING THROUGH DIFFERENT EYES

I want to tell you a story about an African named Juma, a bright and insightful boy. The elders of his village sent him to America to learn their way of thinking and to come back and interpret Western wisdom to the leaders of his village.

A few years later, the young man returned, wearing fine foreign clothing, well educated, and filled with knowledge.

After Juma's return, like all young men in his tribe, he had to pass a test to move into manhood or to become a *warrior,* as they called them in those days. Six elders gathered the nine young men who were eligible for their transition ceremony.

Juma did extremely well until the last day. For the final test, the nine headed deep into the forest, which was half a day's trek from the village. They stopped in front of a large baobab tree. The elders pointed to the tree and, without giving any instructions, walked away from the nine.

Silently the boys surrounded the tree. Two of them wrapped their arms around the trunk. Another reached up and caressed a limb. Four young men chewed its leaves (which are edible and nutritious). The eighth boy stood back, raised his arms, and stared at the tree.

Within minutes, eight of the young men hurried back to the elders. Only Juma remained.

Juma stared at the tree but couldn't figure out what he was supposed to grasp by staring at an old tree. He kept asking himself, *What am I supposed to learn about this tree? What can I tell them that they don't already know?*

He knew it was wrong to ask his peers, so after an hour he went back to the elders. "I do not know what to tell you about the tree," he said. "Please, *wazee* [old men], tell me what I am supposed to learn

111

about the tree."

One old man shook his head. The others wouldn't look at Juma.

The young man went back and stared at the baobab. He sat, he lay on the ground, and several times he circled the tree. He returned to the wazee two more times.

"What is it you want me to see? What information must I bring you about the tree? Tell me."

The wazee sat in silence and would not acknowledge him.

Discouraged and sad, Juma sat next to the baobab tree—a species he had been around all his life. In famine times, he had gathered the leaves for his family to make a delicious soup. Many times he had climbed into the branches of such trees and hidden from his friends.

No matter how hard he tried, however, he could learn nothing new by observing the tree.

The elders sat in a circle, fifty yards away, waiting stoically. He could not find an answer. In frustration, Juma walked to the far side of the tree where the old men were unable to see him. He fell to the ground and cried. "I have failed. I am worthless."

He didn't know what happened next—perhaps he fell asleep or maybe he hallucinated. With a start, he jumped to his feet and impulsively tried to encircle the huge baobab.

He patted the tree fondly. *"Asanti* [thank you]," he said.

He marched proudly up to the wazee, and his face beamed. "I can tell you nothing about the tree; but I can tell you what the tree has spoken to me."

All six elders congratulated Juma. He had passed the test.

It's an old story, but it illustrates a truth. Here in the West, we try to figure out answers by learning facts and analyzing data. Juma's training had helped him analyze, to ask good questions, and he was able to give them information *about* the tree. If asked, he would have been able to explain the many things he'd learned in school.

That wasn't what the elders wanted.

When Juma shifted his way of thinking, the answer came. The people of that village didn't learn by processing vast amounts of knowledge. They learned by going inward and allowing themselves to feel and to hear what was around them.

For them, knowledge was not as important as wisdom. That is, the elders didn't want information; they wanted the young man to have understanding. They wanted him to learn to use his knowledge as a way to understand the tree and thus understand life.

After Juma stopped trying to figure out the answers he assumed the wazee wanted, he was able to move into the realm of wisdom. "I have heard what the tree says to me," Juma said. "I have stopped trying to figure out how to explain the tree."

As I understand this story, Juma's mission had been to go to the West and learn. He was then to come back and translate the wisdom of the educated and enlightened. When Juma returned, he had to relearn the wisdom of the village.

Juma tried to figure out the answers by logical investigation and scrutiny. *He had cut himself off from his inner wisdom.*

That happens to many of us. Perhaps to you as well.

You started with that uninhibited insight about life when you were a child. You spoke out of innocence, and sometimes others laughed at your words, even when you showed insight. The inhibiting forces of society pushed you to deny what you knew.

As I wrote the above, I thought of the tale of the emperor's new clothes. Scammers convinced the king that only people with pure eyes could see the fabulous garments of gold and silver they wove for him. As the word circulated around the kingdom, everyone wanted to be pure, so the people "saw" the magnificent robes.

As the story ends, a small child, seeing the king and royal entourage, yells, "The king is naked." The adults agree and admit they have been self-deceived. The child spoke with "beginner eyes," the perception that hasn't been swayed by prejudice or environment.

On PBS I heard a mystic speak about the *beginner's mind* and urged viewers to cultivate it. If I understood correctly, this means striving to see things without prejudice or from accumulated knowledge, pushing away, or trying to erase the prejudices—positive and negative—to observe people and events as if seeing them for the first time.

That may not be possible, but I like the idea. And I especially like it when it comes to writing.

If you want to write like everyone else, then do nothing differently. Use the same words and speak the same thoughts.

But if you want to enrich others, you have to learn to perceive life differently.

Occasionally I meet individuals who tell me they want to write a great book. They usually say, "I want to write a classic." For them that's a book that sells for generations. They fail in the process. They can't write an insightful book out of what's already known and understood. They must take what they know, look at it from various perspectives, and see it as unique—in a way that others don't see it.

My friend David Morgan once said, "The only original thing you can bring forth that's unique is something you haven't learned." It must be an inner grasp, an understanding that's beyond textbooks and lectures. It's a perception that flows from a source unlike what we call conventional wisdom.

Edgar Allan Poe's poem, "Alone," starts with these words:

From childhood's hour I have not been
As others were; I have not seen
As others saw; I could not bring
My passions from a common spring.

Although Poe wasn't teaching the same lesson I am, his poem embodies what I mean. We read his stories and poetry more than 150 years after his death, and they're still powerful. He perceived life differently from others.

If your writing is to have depth, texture, meaning, and endurance, it must go beyond what others see. That doesn't make you a superior writer, but it does make you different.

None of us sees life through pure lenses. Like everyone else, we filter our insights and the childhood experiences that shaped us. But we don't have to react like anyone else.

If you want to change, you can adjust the way you see things. You can learn to see the naked emperor.

Here's a true account I heard only yesterday, which might make my point clearer. My close friend, whom I'll call Brian, called me after his return from a week-long trip in the Pacific Northwest.

"I used to say I didn't care about money," Brian said, "but I judged everything by money." Over a period of about a year, he became aware of what he called his "poverty mentality," but he didn't know how to be different. In his mind, the impoverished stood against the rich. He scorned the way the wealthy squandered their money.

For his big trip, Brian decided to splurge on business class on the trip west, but he and his wife had to return on coach because no business-class seats were available. Brian's well over six feet tall and wasn't comfortable hunched into the coach class section, but he saved money.

For the outbound trip, he walked into business class "with some misgiving." He'd said many times, "Those people sit in front and, for a few more dollars, they feel superior."

Something happened to Brian on that flight. "Instead of being a victim of overcharge, I was able to sit in the larger, more comfortable seat for five hours and enjoy the ride, the free movies, and the extras."

On his return, Brian and his wife had to leave too early to get breakfast at the hotel. At the airport, he paid eight dollars for each sandwich—the most he'd ever paid for one sandwich. "But I enjoyed eating a tasty meal instead of settling for two tiny packets of peanuts.

"I came from a blue-collar family," he admitted, "and grew up with a chip on my shoulder toward those who had more than I did."

Think about Brian and his new approach to life. He has learned to enjoy life because he discarded his old lenses. It wasn't a lesson about whether to fly business or coach, but it was a lesson about overcoming his prejudice against money and against people who had more than he did.

Like all of us, you have some bias, but you can write with impaired vision. Or you can do what Juma did. You can listen to what your heart tells us and go inward. You can learn to see life differently.

▪ I'VE SPENT MUCH OF MY LIFE BEING LIKE OTHERS. NOW I WANT TO SPEND TIME BEING LIKE THE REAL ME. ▪

23 • EXPANDING YOUR COMFORT ZONE

I had been publishing about ten years when I heard a dynamic speaker at a conference where I taught. He was riveting, and he spoke most of the time about our "comfort zones." At the time, it was a new phrase to me.

"Push ahead! Move on! Take risks!" That's typical of his message. He told several delightful stories of the times he did exactly what he advocated and gave us the marvelous results—all success stories.

I liked what he said, and I bought a CD. He was inspiring. I wanted to push against the boundaries and restrictions of my life.

But after I heard the CD at home, a number of questions surfaced. The first one was simple: What happens if I step out of my comfort zone and fail?

Had he ever failed? If so, how did it affect him? If he didn't fail, was he embracing risks or simply taking the next obvious step?

As a writer, I've taken risks and some have succeeded; others haven't. For example, I've earned most of my income as a ghostwriter or collaborator. Each time I take on a project it's a risk, and I move out of what I know and feel comfortable with.

In 2003, I wrote a proposal for a book called *90 Minutes in Heaven.* I believed in the book, and so did my agent. But it was a risk in many ways. Don Piper attended two writers' conferences and pitched the book himself. He found no interest. My agent got turndowns from about a dozen publishers.

But I believed in the book. I truly had a sense that the book would be big (although it turned out to be bigger than I had believed). Despite the rejections, I couldn't drop it.

We finally sold *90 Minutes in Heaven* to Revell, part of Baker Books. As of this writing, the book has sold in excess of five million copies in English, and the last I heard, it had gone into forty-one translations.

That's history, but what about the risk factor? Had I really moved out of my comfort zone? According to that charismatic speaker, I hadn't.

I could obviously argue this either way, but from my perspective, I stayed with the book because I believed in it. I trusted my instincts, and I've been wrong a few times. I didn't see it as risky, only as the way the publishing business operates.

"Take the next right step" is the way a woman named Tracy said in my Sunday school class—and she referred to something else, but the principle was correct. Those words stayed with me and became a kind of mantra for moving ahead.

The charismatic speaker had urged us to push ourselves, to march forward against the odds. "Dream big," he said and implored us to take those dreams and fight the forces of doubt until we prevailed.

That method may work—but it's not my style. And that's what I want to emphasize. It may not be your style, either.

You hear or read intriguing information, get excited about projects or ideas, and you don't do anything about them. The tendency is to feel you've failed or you've procrastinated.

Maybe.

Or perhaps it's your inner wisdom that pulls you back and refuses to let you participate. Here's an example of what I mean. I own six books on how to make a lot of money through marketing books. Four of them sold big among writers, because they were on an important topic. One promised a thousand ways to sell our tomes, another assured us that if we followed his unconventional techniques, it would pay off. I have yet to try any of those sure-fire, success-guaranteed ideas.

For a long time I occasionally castigated myself because I didn't jump on the things other writers did. I belonged to two writers' loops, and they kept throwing out marketing ideas that couldn't fail. They seemed to have so many excellent ideas, and I felt insecure because I didn't do what they did.

One day a thought rammed itself into my head. *I don't do what they do, but I'm successful; they do what they say, but most of them aren't successful.*

Even the espoused, absolutely certain tactics didn't work for all of them. Here's an example of what I mean. One woman boasts she always carries at least two copies of her book when she travels, and she's on planes a minimum of four times a month.

She initiates a conversation with whoever sits next to her. "That person doesn't get off the plane without a copy of my book," she says. "It's wonderful advertising."

I can't do that. I *wouldn't* do that.

Do I think she's wrong? If it works for her, that may be all right. I couldn't do it because such a tactic goes against my style and my integrity. One time someone like that woman sat next to me on a long flight. He talked and talked, despite my frequent looking away or pulling a book out of my laptop case. His product was vitamins, and he was sure I wouldn't stay healthy if I didn't take them.

He kept trying to push his product by telling me everything it cured. "I don't have that problem," I said repeatedly.

The man went on to some other, probably hidden disease. I picked up a book and tried to read, but he kept talking. I finally said, "First, I'm boringly healthy with no physical problems. I take no meds—only some vitamin supplements."

That was my mistake. When he found out the company from which I bought my vitamins, he was nice about it but insisted his company's products were superior.

He yakked for close to an hour until I finally said, "I'm really not interested, and I would like to read."

"Oh, sure, of course. I wouldn't want to distract you."

I didn't reply. I didn't want to get into another discussion with him about distractions.

I provide these two illustrations because I assume that method works for both of those salespeople. It doesn't fit into my sense of integrity. It would go against my inner values to push people. Perhaps that's why I've never been in sales.

Here's my position, and I offer it to you: Start within your comfort zone and write from who you are. That's not all. I urge you to begin what I call an *unrelenting search for your true self.* As you learn about yourself, you expand your comfort zone. You take what some would call risks, but to you the so-called risk becomes the next right step.

At least that's how it's often been with me.

■ ■ ■

I'm a strong advocate of operating from your superior mode. That is, as you learn who you are, you make decisions and take actions that are commensurate with your personality.

Too many people try to operate out of their inferior mode because they're taught to behave in a certain manner, and they assume it's correct. They're uncomfortable but feel they must do it "the right way."

By superior and inferior modes, I mean that you have an operating system. When you work from your inner values, you have confidence, but more than that, you don't feel deceptive, manipulative, or uncomfortable.

I'll explain it this way. I have three bank accounts—one personal and two for business. Each month I balance my books. Once in a while, after I've posted all expenses and incomes, my figures agree with the bank's balance. Most of the time, however, it takes about thirty minutes because, even with a calculator, I have to add and re-add everything. Thus, working with numbers means working with my inferior mode.

When writing, it's painful for me to think about writing for teens, and I couldn't conceive of my doing a book about science.

We're all different. When you push yourself or move from an inferior or defensive position, you're under stress. You tend to be less than your best. And in writing, it becomes lesser-quality. It may be safe writing, but it's often flat. Or what I call *derivative writing.*

There is only one right way—your way. When you act out of who you are, you can't go wrong. I'm enthusiastic and excitable—passionate—and I talk about this in Chapter 26. I also am committed not to bore others or overwhelm them to do things a particular way.

To go back to the comfort zone analogy, my question is simple: What's wrong with staying in your present zone? If you're aware of yourself, your situation, and if you're connected to your inner motivation, do you need more?

Do you need to push forward or march onward? Do you need to go on the attack?

I don't, and I don't want to be a role model that says, "Do it my way."

If I become a model for anyone, I want to be one who not only gives permission but urges others to do things their way.

• MOVING OUT OF MY COMFORT ZONE IS RIGHT WHEN IT'S THE NEXT BEST STEP, OR IF IT FITS WITHIN MY SUPERIOR MODE. •

24 · COMPARING YOURSELF

I n the 1988 vice-presidential debates, Dan Quayle, a Republican, compared himself to President John F. Kennedy. Lloyd Bentsen responded, "Senator, I knew Jack Kennedy, and you're not Jack Kennedy."

That simple statement, although sometimes slightly altered, has become part of our culture. It's a way to warn people from comparing themselves too favorably with someone more accomplished.

Occasionally I hear writers compare themselves. "I write better than…"

What I think each time, without saying it, is, *And how do you prove that?*

I understand those who make such claims. I did it a few times early in my career. I wish someone had corrected me (or maybe I really don't). The one instance that stays in my memory was when we were in a small group and someone mentioned a much-published author and I said, "I write better than she does." No one argued or agreed, and the discussion went on to another topic.

I'd be too embarrassed to make that statement today. I don't excuse myself, but I think I understand now what was going on then. I had started publishing, received positive responses, and assumed I knew more about the craft than I truly did.

I was like the young stag who challenges the dominant buck of the herd. He feels stronger and more able, but he may be too optimistic.

I suspect that most of us who write seriously have found at least one or two occasions when we've favorably weighed our self-perception against someone else's published works. "I can do better than that."

If this sounds like you, it's more than boasting. It may be a stage of growth and mean you've grown enough to see weaknesses in others' writing.

At least that was true for me. As I continued to learn better writing practices, I became hypercritical of what I read. Eventually I figured out that even though I might write clearer sentences or better descriptions, that didn't make me superior. It meant I had figured out better techniques. Because I had worked diligently on one or two finer points—areas some writers hadn't learned—it was easy to feel superior.

The self-inflated contrast is probably far less difficult to cope with and overcome than negative comparison.

When I use positive and negative, I refer to the result of comparing. Neither is good for you. If you're constantly seeing yourself as better, it probably means you have no idea how bad your writing truly is. (If you don't like *bad*, try *weak*.)

When you place your manuscript alongside another's and see yourself negatively, the result can be demoralizing. You might become discouraged and say, "I'll never write that well."

Comparison—regardless of the result—can be deadly. You can't win. You either become smug and complacent, or you go the other way and feel depressed and despairing.

If you feel you're weaker or inferior, but you determine to continue, you may try to imitate those you label "superior writers."

I know: I've done that as well.

Afterward, I decided that, although they were probably better, and I didn't want to consciously imitate them, I would still read some of them.

I stumbled on a technique that I found helpful, and I pass it on. When I read one book by an author and like the writing, I search for everything that person has written. I buy them or borrow them from the library.

I start with the earliest-written book. It amazes me to observe the growth of the writer from book to book, especially after the first.

Two things I've learned from that: That person who seemed so advanced and excellent didn't start with great skills. The first book or two showed promise, but the author seemed to need to produce four or five volumes before reaching the quality level that I appreciated.

Seeing their early works (and especially their weaknesses) enables me to say to myself, "I can grow. I can become better."

■ ■ ■

Will you ever stop comparing and contrasting? Perhaps not, but you can learn to do it differently. You can do what I call *an appreciative evaluation.*

Comparing yourself with well-known writers isn't the real issue. A friend read the latest book by Malcolm Gladwell, and he wanted to sell books with that kind of easy-read, commonsense advice. "But I'm no Malcolm Gladwell," he said.

"The world needs only one Gladwell," I said, "and he beat you for that honor. The position is filled."

After he laughed, I added, "You're not in competition with him or any other writer."

He moaned about the fact that he couldn't lay out his material as simply and clearly. Again I stopped him. "Gladwell is *not* your competition. His success or ability has nothing to do with you."

I went on to point out, "You have only one person with whom to compete: *yourself.* You can improve, you can learn, but you can't be Gladwell."

As long as you focus on the superstars of prose, you'll feel inferior. But if you work to strengthen yourself and to become the best you are at what you write, you can't lose.

One day I figured out what to do to help myself. As I studied my writing, I reminded myself what people said about the good points— and I chose to ignore the critics.

This is important for me to make clear. I wanted to focus on the things I did well. And the primary way for me to figure out my positive characteristics was to pay attention to the compliments.

Or here's the way I say it: Discover what you do well and do more of it; many writers learn what they do badly and do more of it. I wanted to capitalize on what I did well. I promised myself also to try to improve in the areas of weakness—which I had to face—but not to focus heavily on them. I also realized that, in some areas, I'll probably always be weak.

I'll illustrate that by pointing to my two daughters. Wanda was a top student with excellent grades. I never worried about her. Cecile, however, was the artistic type, and she stayed in the average category in the subjects where her older sister excelled.

One time, Cecile had a low report grade in social studies. I asked one question: "Did you do your best?"

With tears in her eyes, she nodded.

"That's all I ask." And I meant that. When it came to music and art, she was outstanding, so she had her areas of strength. She would never pull down the grades that put her sister on the honor roll.

It works the same way with writing. You can't be perfect; you won't be outstanding in every phase of the craft. Here's your primary question: Am I doing my best? If you can answer yes, you're further along than the average writer.

Here are my self-scrutiny questions. They may aid your progress.

- What are my strengths?
- How can I make them even stronger?
- What kind of things do I write well?
- Where am I weak?
- In what areas do I need improvement?

Simple questions, but I pushed myself to look inward as honestly as I could. Although difficult for me, I was able to see and acknowledge my strengths.

I want to point out two of my better qualities. I don't do that to imply others aren't stronger in these areas (and certainly some weaker). I also write this not to compare myself with others.

First, *I write with "heart."* At least that's how several people have described my style. Readers tell me they can feel what I write. That's probably my greatest strength. People who know me say, "When I read you, I feel you're sitting on the sofa next to me, and we're talking."

Here's what I consider one of the highest compliments from a woman I met at a conference: "I liked you just from reading your books. Now that I've met you in person, I like you even more."

I try not to condescend or to talk over their heads. When I write, I want to feel I'm staring into their eyes and saying, "This is what I believe, and I want to share this with you to enrich your life."

Second, *I write with clarity.* That is, I seem able to take complicated issues or thoughts and make them simple.

I wrote *Gifted Hands* for Dr. Ben Carson, and it appeared in print in 1990. In that book, I had to describe CT scans and MRIs. In 1990, the general public wasn't familiar with either term. Or at least I wasn't, and if I don't know something, I assume there are others like me.

My research indicated that a British doctor invented the CT scan in the 1970s, and it took years before it became the common medical tool we use today.

If I wrote lengthy paragraphs to describe the CT scan, I'd bore readers. If I used technical jargon, I'd lose their concentration. Here was my question: How could I explain a CT scan in one sentence? Remember, when I wrote *Gifted Hands,* personal computers had barely come on the scene, and none of us had heard of hard drives, icons, and the World Wide Web.

I struggled over that definition for a long time. Here's what I finally wrote and inserted as a footnote: "Commonly called Cat Scans for Computerized Tomography, this is a highly technical, sophisticated computer that allows X-ray beams to focus at different levels."[15]

How much more did readers need to know? I felt I provided a basic understanding for that kind of book, Ben Carson's autobiography.

---

[15] *Gifted Hands: The Ben Carson Story.* Ben Carson, M.D., with Cecil Murphey (Grand Rapids, MI: Zondervan, 1990) 126, footnote.

The only healthy way to compare your writing is to look at *your* earlier work and contrast it with your current products. I rarely read anything of my own after it's in print, unless I'm going to be interviewed about it, so it's not something I liked doing.

Recently, however, my agent decided to put some of my out-of-print books into ebook format. Her decision forced me to read eight books written more than twenty years ago and to write new introductions. In all candor, some of my bad writing shocked me. By bad, I mean such things as weak sentences or places where my syntax was awkward.

But once in a while I read what I call a *gem*—a sentence or a paragraph where I said aloud, "This isn't bad." (I really meant, "This is good.")

By comparing myself with myself, I saw that I had grown. As painful as it was to see what I got away with out of ignorance, it also encouraged me to say, "I was able to get published when I wrote that badly, and I know I've improved since those days."

I'm better now than I was when I wrote those books in the early 1980s. That's the kind of comparison in which I believe.

> ■ IF I EVALUATE MY WRITING,
> I COMPARE MY OLDER WORK WITH MY NEWER
> SO I CAN SEE MY GROWTH. ■

25 · OUR ENVIOUS NATURE

My writer friend Hoss told me that he absolutely refuses to go to the annual booksellers trade shows, even when he has a newly released book and he could do signings.

"When I look at the thousands of books on display, I hate it," he said. "I envy them their success."

That was certainly honest—and perhaps more honest than many would be. And envy is a common writer malady.

Years ago, for instance, I headed a group called the Scribe Tribe. We were all in the early phases of our publishing careers. Several of us had our first articles accepted during that time together, and none of us had reached the book-publishing stage.

Marion Bond West and I were the two most prolific members. Each time the Scribe Tribe met, we started with a brief report of our literary activities. Few meetings took place in which neither of us reported an acceptance or a publication. Occasionally both of us also reported our rejections.

I'm not sure how it began, but one time I watched the others' facial responses. When I reported a rejection, they were kind and sympathetic. They seemed amazingly kind not only with their words, but I could see it in their eyes.

When either Marion or I mentioned a success, they smiled. But the smile muscles of several Scribe-Tribers seemed to work only around the mouth. Their eyes didn't reflect joy or excitement.

One evening I reported on the sale of a magazine article to an editor who asked me to send him more because he liked my style. I don't remember Marion's report, but it seems to me that she had sold two articles to *Guidepost*.

I believe they tried to express joy over our achievements, but the other six couldn't make it convincing. That's when I realized a significant fact: *They're envious.*

That hadn't occurred to me before. Even as the awareness came, I didn't see why they should feel envious. But then, they probably weren't sure either. Maybe they weren't aware.

Their emotion was more than comparing themselves with Marion and me. I sensed they wanted *our* success and perhaps even inwardly detested us for our achievements. If I had mentioned envy, I'm sure they would have vehemently denied it.

I never brought it up, but after that I shared fewer of my publication successes.

The emotion of envy is there—and it's not unique. Probably most of us struggle with it on some level.

Although we tend to interchange *envy* and *jealousy*, I'm convinced they're different. Here's how I make the distinction, although both are negative emotions. Jealousy happens when we're focused on another person. I may be jealous if you spend too much time with someone I love.

Let's say I invited my agent, Deidre Knight, to have lunch with a group of writers. You're a good friend, so you sit across from Deidre and me. For the next hour, you ignore me, but you keep a steady stream of conversation going with Deidre. I feel *jealous* of the attention she's receiving and of the rejection or indifference you show me.

Envy is different. It's not focused the same way. For me, envy doesn't want you to have it because I want it myself *and only for myself.* I can be envious of any writer who is more successful, has a better platform, hosts a bigger Web presence, or gets more tweets than I do. That means I want what she has.

Envy is often mentioned in Catholic moral theology as one of the seven deadly sins. And if envy grabs you, you might resent anyone who seems to have more or something better than you do. If unchecked, envy can lead to loathing the other.

I know the affliction personally. I became aware of a writer who has been publishing less than five years, has several books (none of them in my field), but has attracted attention. People seem to speak with awe when his name emerges in conversation.

I envied him.

It seemed as if I had worked hard for years, slowly and finally achieved; he worked less hard (or at least fewer years) and quickly achieved. *I wanted the recognition and appreciation he had received.*

That's how I see envy at work. Most writers seem to stumble over that "deadly sin" at some point. So if you become a victim, don't be surprised.

The gravity of the sickness obviously depends on how strongly you feel. You might recognize that you're envious and bewail your weakness or human failing—which probably comes out of your childhood need for affirmation and acceptance. That's how I finally understood envy.

I wanted. I wanted. I wanted.

When someone else got what I wanted, I battled within myself. I condemned myself for being so weak because I lusted for what the other person had.

I've moved beyond that phase but not without serious struggles.

The most obvious way I see envy working is through disparaging remarks about others' writing. It's an old problem of elevating ourselves by tearing down someone else.

I see so much envy within publishing. No one has ever said to me, "I envy him and wish I had his success." But their actions shout what their lips conceal.

I think of the time "Jean" and I sat next to each other at the opening session of a conference in Southern California. The keynote speaker mentioned that one of his books had sold nearly two million copies, and he had received word that a famous actor had purchased the film rights.

Jean leaned over and whispered, "I don't understand why people buy his trashy novels. They're empty of content with boring prose that almost puts me to sleep."

That's what she said; that's not what she meant.

I couldn't read her mind, but here's my take on that remark. If Jean had been aware of her true feelings (and I'm only assuming she wasn't), she might have said, "I work faithfully, and my books don't even earn back their advances. Everything he writes goes into hundreds of thousands of copies. I want his level of success."

I don't have a long list of answers to envy, and I assume it's a natural response, especially when we're not as successful as we want to be. Is anyone ever successful enough?

If it afflicts you, it probably means you're heavily committed to becoming the best possible writer and that other authors—undeserving in your opinion—get the acclaim that should be yours.

Think about this scenario. You work hard. You learn everything you can through instruction books, conferences, and reading other writers. Perhaps you've taken one or two online courses. You have a mentor or a group of friends who edit your work. You doggedly focus on becoming the best.

You meet another author who achieves more success than you do. "I work hard and get no payback," you might say to yourself. "She halfheartedly pursues the craft, and she's successful. That's not fair."

It may not be, but whoever said life was fair? That kind of thing happens.

The other author enjoys the success of a highly acclaimed first book or a million-copies-sold of a third volume, while you plod away trying to write one that sells more than eight thousand copies.

Why wouldn't you fight envy? Why wouldn't you feel hurt that you work diligently, faithfully, and still achieve little? You handle your envy by what I call sideways remarks.

- "I tried to read two of her books. I couldn't finish either."
- "It's hard for me to believe that people actually *buy* his books."
- "I keep thinking she'll improve, but the quality stays in the basement, and I haven't seen any improvement."
- "You mean you enjoy reading such mediocrity? Or is calling his work *mediocre* a compliment?"

Snide. Petty. Unkind. Those statements in themselves may not be too serious; however, if you listen to your words, you know envy has taken over. Remember the adage that goes, "If you can't say something nice, don't say anything"? That adage is still good advice.

Because I've been in this writing life longer than most writers who still produce and sell, I'd like to tell you how I see this problem capturing the heart of writers. I'll also suggest a few possible solutions.

First, *envy is natural.* It's not a moral failure or a flaw in your character. In fact, it says you're aware of yourself, as well as being conscious of others. It says you care deeply about the craft, and you want to succeed.

Second, there is a positive element. *You can use that emotion to push you to improve your writing style.* The negative occurs when you allow your attitude or actions to divert your energy.

Third, *once you're aware of envy, you have a choice.* You can encourage it to grow by giving it tacit permission. The most obvious way is to speak up *unfavorably* every time you hear the other's name mentioned.

Now let's look at what you can do to stop envy from growing in your heart.

First, *say nothing negative* about other writers, no matter how strongly you feel. You may tell yourself that you're only being objective—and maybe you are. But you also may be feeding the demon called envy.

Here's a second tip. Years ago I heard the statement, "*Fake it until you make it.*" At the time I rejected it, but I've found it useful. You might try it. It has worked for me.

Suppose you think, *Cec Murphey must feel he's a big shot and knows more than anyone else. What audacity for him to write a book for writers.* But because you're aware, you remind yourself, *I wish I could have the success he has enjoyed.*

When my name comes up in conversation, you can say something simple such as, "He's been at the craft a long time." "He's earned his success." They don't have to be words of lavish praise, but honest statements that take little effort.

Third, if you're a praying person, *pray for the other writer.* If I were praying for Cec Murphey, I'd say something direct, such as, "God, enable me to accept him as he is. I accept his level of achievement." You might have to pray it daily for a long time, but try it.

Your goal is not to think of me as your best friend, but to accept my achievement level as having no effect on your career. If you can accept my accomplishments, you benefit by becoming a stronger, healthier person and possibly a better writer.

Now you can focus on your craft without wishing you were somebody else who has attained what you consider the epitome of triumph—the kind of feat you yearn to experience.

I have one final suggestion to help you deal with envy. Ask yourself this question: *What am I learning about myself through this emotional reaction?*

It can enable you to be aware of what's important to you. Would you envy someone in areas about which you care nothing? Are you envious of NFL running backs or scientists who win Nobel prizes?

Envy strikes at your heart—your desires. If you're aware that you envy another writer, let that be a message of how important it is to you to achieve, to succeed in your writing goals.

Perhaps that seems obvious, but I want to tell you about my friend Wayne. He wrote six articles, and they sold. He wrote several more, and they sold. He wrote a book, and it didn't sell. Fifteen editors and five agents turned him down.

One day he said to me, "If I didn't like you so much, I'd hate you." After we both laughed, he told me that he had begun to resent me. "You seem to write anything you want and succeed at it. You write a proposal, and your agent sells it. You work on another book, and the same thing happens."

After Wayne had released his negative-but-honest feelings, I could have pointed out the hard work I do or the hours I spend in front of my computer screen. I could have emphasized the number of years I've been learning this craft. I could also have mentioned my rejections that he didn't know about.

But logic and reasoning weren't the answer. So, instead, I leaned forward. "But think about what you told me. It shows me that you care deeply about writing. From things I've heard you say in the past, I felt you were a dilettante—a dabbler—and success in publishing seemed like a hobby and didn't mean much."

He admitted that his writing had begun that way. "Now I care, and I'm afraid to let people know how much success means to me."

One of the last things I said to him, which he reminded me of a year later, was this: "There are two kinds of envy. It can be malicious, undermining, resentful, and you feel there's no justice in the world because I've attained what you want.

"Or there is a benign, admiring kind of envy. It means you want to achieve what I have. And you're willing to work hard to make it happen."

> **▪ I CAN RESENT OTHERS FOR THEIR ACHIEVEMENTS, OR I CAN ADMIRE THEM FOR WHAT THEY'VE ACCOMPLISHED. I CAN DETERMINE TO WORK AS HARD AS THEY DO. ▪**

26 · WRITING-YOUR PASSION

Twelve of us writers had lunch together at a conference. I sat next to "Mike," whom I didn't know well. Years earlier I had read one of his books, but I hadn't remembered much about the content.

He was enthusiastic, and I enjoyed listening to him. Somewhere in the conversation, he talked about sending out proposals.

"I find them difficult to write," I said. "I do them because that's what publishers want, but I'm not good on the marketing aspect of the proposals, yet I do great on the rest of it."

He told me how easy it was for him to write proposals. "Right now I have thirty-four proposals out to publishers."

"Thirty-four?" I couldn't believe what I heard.

He smiled and nodded. He told me proudly that all of them had gone out during the past three months.

"How can you be passionate about thirty-four ideas? Over a period of years, but months—"

"I'm a passionate guy," he said and moved on to another subject.

I was stuck on the thirty-four proposals and kept thinking about his offhand remark for a couple of days. At that same conference, I was in a conversation with an agent and an editor. I mentioned Mike.

"We refuse to look at anything by him," the editor said. "He sends us so many bad proposals, it's not worth sifting to find something worthwhile."

The agent said she had turned down representing him twice. "Every time he has a thought about anything," she said, "he feels driven to write it. I've never seen any seriously thought-out thing from him."

Then I understood Mike; I also understood a little more about the importance of passion. No one can be passionate about thirty-four concepts—perhaps over a period of time, but not within months, and certainly not all at the same time.

I'm prolific, but I wouldn't have more than a dozen solid ideas to propose in a single year. That's not to make me the example, only to say that I'm probably typical.

Something else that fits along this line is a question I hear many writers ask agents and editors: "What kind of books are you looking for?"

I don't ask that question, and it has no relevance for me. I don't care what they're looking for; I care about what I have to offer. If I'm not passionate about a topic, or can't become fervent, I don't want to give it serious consideration.

Think about that question the ambitious authors ask: "What kind of books are *you* looking for?" The implication is that if editors start listing what they seek, the writer's response would be, "Oh, I could write that for you."

Maybe the writer could, but is it a topic over which they can infuse zeal and pleasure? Is it something that fascinates them and will keep them excited for months?

The time element is significant, because most people can stay excited about something for a week. Maybe a month. But how about long-term passion? How about long enough to write a book?

I asked one agent the general question, "How long does it take the average writer to complete a full book?"

"Although it depends on the genre and the writer," she said, "I'd estimate nine months."

Nine months, or even if they could do it in six, that means most writers need a topic that sustains interest and keeps the energy flowing. I'm a fast writer, and it's not so much the length of time, but I tend to bog down about the midpoint (which I've discussed earlier). I don't stop writing, but I have to fight to believe I'm doing a credible job. The self-doubts nag at me.

My point is that unless the excitement drives them, many quit before completing the project.

I have a friend who has started more than twenty novels. I read the first four chapters of a delightful book he started. I liked it so much I showed his proposal to my agent. His writing style and storyline fascinated her. I told her of his history and she said, "If he finishes the entire novel and the writing stays at this level, I'd love to read it for possible representation."

I told him the news, which excited and motivated him.

That was in 2007. I didn't hear from him for about three years. In our last conversation, he mentioned his new novel.

"What about...?"

"Oh that? It started out all right, but I lost interest."

Beyond the matter of passion to keep you going when your inner resources slow down or dry up, unless you sustain fervency, your book won't be strong, and you might quit before you reach the last page.

Your attitude toward your project shows through. I suppose some people write books strictly for the money—at least they say they do—but is money really enough? Surely, the motivation has to be stronger.

Here's an example. A decade ago, a wealthy entrepreneur in Southern California offered me $200,000 a year to be his in-residence writer. I would produce books exclusively for him and would carry my byline below his. "I have twenty-nine books I want to write, and I'll pay the yearly amount until you finish them." He told me about half a dozen of his ideas, offered to provide all the research I needed, as well as a new, top-quality computer and printer.

I turned him down. I felt no enthusiasm. No conviction. His book ideas were topics on which I probably had only a mild interest. Although none of the ideas went against my sense of integrity, I had no strong feelings to pursue them. That question of zeal or passion was the deciding factor.

Conviction and energy come from within. Your fervency (or lack of it) shows, whether you're writing about investing in stocks, historical fiction, or how to build a fabulous wardrobe on a budget.

To write passionately, you need to "catch fire," as one writer put it. You need to be carried along by something stronger than your normal self. When you consider writing a book on any topic, check your feelings. Ask yourself, "Can I stay excited about this for nine months or a year?"

When I'm physically with someone, I tend to get excited when the person proposes an idea. Perhaps that comes from my years as a ghostwriter—to encourage and elicit their feelings. But no matter how enthusiastic I am, rarely do I agree to write on the spot.

I've learned a better way. Usually I say that I want to think, pray, ponder it first. If I'm still excited a week later, that's a strong indication of passion. But often after I'm away from the person, my excitement drops from 100 percent to about 20. That's not high enough for me to undertake a writing project.

Here's something I do: "If I'm writing this book," I say to myself, "I'm unavailable to write anything else. Is this idea good enough to make me say no to an exciting project?"

Here's another tip that, for me, fits in with this concept of passion. The work itself—the writing of the words—needs to be its own reward.

This isn't some abstract, intellectual jargon. The words, often private, intrinsic, and subjective have to satisfy that "something" within you.

Writing passionately fulfills certain inward demands. If you don't find pleasure in typing the words and thoughts, you're not writing from passion.

When you write, you probably start with what you've thought about, know, or you've researched, but that's not where fervor enters the process. Passion flows when you discover what you didn't yet know. It's like finding a wrapped gift at your front door with your name on it, and you can hardly wait to open the box.

One woman called writing an "excavation." Sentence by sentence, what she needed to say came out of vast searching in underground caverns (her inner self).

I like her words. I write for self-discovery, and the writing doesn't have to be subjective. If writing is excavating, you learn deeper meanings, and the intensity increases through the simple act of tapping the keyboard.

Serious Bible readers understand this. They'll read a portion of the Good Book several times, but one day a sentence or a thought leaps out at them. It's probably true with certain kinds of poetry. Usually it's a personal message they need that day, even if it's not in the same context as the original version.

Here's an example. I had agreed to ghostwrite for a man and I liked the idea, but one chapter was about something with which I didn't agree. It was one of those things that's a matter of point of view and not a truth-versus-error issue. Even so, I couldn't seem to write. Yet I had signed a contract to do it and didn't want to say, "Sorry..."

One morning I was reading in the Psalms and honestly not thinking about the book. I read Psalm 15 that asks a question about those who are worthy of God's presence. The next four verses answer, and right in the middle I read the words that they "keep their promises even when it hurts."[16]

I had the answer. I had focused on my difficulty and my not liking his position. I had forgotten something even more important: my promise, my oath, my contract.

I closed my eyes and thanked God. I learned something about myself and faced the reality. I thought of the words my dad used to say: "A man's word is his bond." From that moment on, the zeal to write—the excitement I hadn't found—swept in. It was his book, and I felt a great impassioned power to make it the best I could for him.

· I AM A PASSIONATE PERSON. I CAN BE A PASSIONATE WRITER IF I CHOOSE. ·

---

[16] Psalm 15:4

27 · LETTING IT GO

Sometimes I classify writers as those who won't hold back their manuscripts, and those who won't let go of them.

Too many writers are so anxious they can't wait. They *must* release their manuscripts. And most of the times, it's before they're ready.

The first—those who have to send everything as soon as they hit the final period—are more resistant to help. I'll talk about them first.

My opinion is that the more insecure you are, the more you'll refuse to learn and grow. You'll defend obvious mistakes or be unable to hear criticism. If this applies to you, that means you must be right when you discuss anything. You can't face being wrong, and you rarely apologize.

For example, I'll tell you about a therapist I'll call Dan. Although we had met years earlier, after he learned I had become a full-time writer, he phoned me. We talked quite a bit, but several times Dan said, "I want to get published."

He didn't say he wanted to learn to write or get better, only to get into print. Perhaps I should have caught on, but I didn't. I told him I had formed a small group of writers who met regularly, and I invited him to join us.

Eagerly he joined us. I read his first article and the information was all right, but he didn't write well. Every paragraph had at least one sentence using the passive voice—and he could easily have changed that and enlivened his writing. There were other weaknesses, but that seemed the most glaring.

I marked on his manuscript before we met. In our meeting we gave each other brief oral critiques, and when Dan's turn came I said, "You make your writing flabby with the passive voice. Your prose sounds as if you want readers to stay about four feet away and not get too close."

139

Dan nodded in agreement as I talked, but he said nothing. The others affirmed my reaction.

The next time Dan sent in his manuscript, I didn't see improvement. "One of the first rules of good writing," I said to him at our meeting, "is to avoid the passive voice." I stressed *avoid* and went on to explain several instances where he might want to use it.

He nodded and didn't argue.

The third manuscript was virtually the same as the two previous. Instead of jumping at everything, I focused on his extensive use of the passive voice. I explained to him why it was weak and also what I meant by the term. "Do you understand what I mean by passive voice?"

"Yes, I do."

"Why do you keep using it?"

"I like the passive voice."

That remark slammed the door in my face. It was his way of saying he wasn't teachable. That's when I understood what he meant by "getting published." He didn't want to improve, only to get in print.

He didn't return to our group.

I want to share what I've learned from working with individuals like Dan. They want shortcuts or magic formulas, but they don't want to work at learning to write. They want to sell, not improve.

If you're still reading, I assume you're not like Dan. Or at least you try not to be like him. Early in my career, I sometimes resisted correction. I couldn't handle the idea that my writing wasn't good, especially after I had created and corrected multiple drafts and had been edited by my peer group. I learned not only to accept corrections but I learned from them.

Over the years I've encountered too many want-to-be successful authors who seem to feel entitled to have their manuscripts accepted regardless of the quality or their lack of skills. Their attitude implies, "I've written it, so I know it's good."

I think of a man who attended a conference in Colorado for several years. I met him at five of them. He determined to sell his five-hundred-page manuscript. Each year he clutched the same manuscript and without making a single change.

"I know this is good," he said to me more than once. "I just need to find the right editor or agent." So every year he showed the same manuscript to any professional who would look at it.

I don't know the result, but I assume he finally gave up.

The second group is the one I want to address—they're like me, or at least the way I used to be. And my problem wasn't as serious as many others who don't want to release their manuscripts. They're the writers who hold back their manuscripts and have problems releasing them.

Does that describe you?

Somewhere I read about the "Branwell Brontë Syndrome." Charlotte, Emily, and Anne Brontë were three sisters who all published in the early nineteenth century, which was quite amazing. Their only brother, Branwell, also had writing aspirations but never published. He tried a number of occupations and failed in all of them. He became a slave to opium and alcohol.

Years ago, in a biography of the family, Branwell said that he couldn't stand the idea of an editor destroying his writing by throwing it into the fire. No one knows if he was a good or bad writer, and he died at age thirty-one.

A wasted life. Wasted talent. If only he had sent his work to an editor, but he never did.

You may be a talented author who carries the same emotions. You want to release your writing, but you can't.

Here's my worst example of working with someone like that. Twenty years ago a publisher came to Atlanta to see two of us writers. He wanted us to collaborate on a project. Both of us agreed. A month later, we had the contract and signed it. The book would carry both of our bylines.

It wasn't a happy relationship. My co-writer promised to have work done on a particular day and didn't honor that self-imposed deadline. Not once. Tired of pushing my co-writer, I did about 80 percent of the book before he finally gave me a few chapters.

Two weeks before I mailed in the completed manuscript, he wrote a letter to me and to our editor. "Please take my name off the book," he said. His explanation was that he believed everything he wrote, "But in a year I may change, and my writing would then be invalid."

I phoned him and tried to reason with him. "We're all learning. We modify things and, in fact, that's part of growth. We write what we know right now and believe at this moment."

He wouldn't change his mind, so the book went to press with only my name. I believed then, and I still believe, that wasn't his real reason. I don't think he could bear to issue his work in public, under his name. In his opinion, the writing wasn't good enough. That is, it wasn't perfect.

I've met others like him. They simply can't let go. On the whole, I'm long past that stage, but it wasn't easy. I knew my writing was all right, but I was also smart enough to realize it could be better.

The problem? I didn't know how to make it better.

If I held the manuscript for a few weeks or months, I'd absorb more about the craft and the present project would be better. The fallacy of that thinking is it means either constantly revising as I learn more or waiting until I have it "all worked out," which means I wouldn't release my writing.

I'm not a perfectionist, but it was painful to release an article or book. I would think, *This could be better.* However, I didn't know how to make it better.

I'm highly prolific, and one reason is because I finally figured out how to say to myself, "This is the best I can do at this stage of my development."

Every day for about two weeks I would repeat the sentence several times: "This is the best I can do at this stage of my development."

That's true, because it is.

I finally gave myself permission to let go. When I write anything, and I know it's the best I can do *right now*, I repeat my simple statement: "This is the best I can do at this stage of my development."

142

In my career as a ghostwriter-collaborator I've had only two people who wouldn't let go. The more difficult one was the late Norman Vaughan, then the last-surviving member of Admiral Byrd's historic trip to Antarctica in 1928–1930. We had sold the book, and the contract gave us a deadline. We agreed to meet it.

Norman had so many stories to tell of his sixty-year career, he kept giving me new material. Several times I said, "Norm, we have enough."

He agreed, but a few days later he'd have more to add. The deadline was drawing closer, but Norm didn't slow down.

Finally, I phoned our editor and pleaded, "Please tell Norm not to send in more stories." I suggested she contact him and tell him to save them for a second book.

She did. Norm got that message and stopped.

Several times Norm told me that he felt the book was good, but he wanted to make it better. His way to make it better was to add, add, add. My way to make it better was to do a good job on the material we had and stop.

If you're the kind who holds back, who wants to make it "just a little better," take a big risk.

Let it go.

Perhaps you need to repeat my words until you're able to release your writing.

· THIS IS THE BEST I CAN DO AT THIS STAGE OF MY DEVELOPMENT. ·

A PARTING WORD
FROM CECIL MURPHEY

So, why *do* you want to write? What pushes or compels you to keep on writing? Even in the midst of uncertainty, rejections, and inner and outer critics of your work?

You don't have to write—and life might be easier for you if you delete all your document files.

But if you feel you *must* write—if you *know* you'll never be fulfilled unless you give it your best—you'll be miserable if you delete those files.

As I wrote that last sentence, I thought of a poem that has stayed with me since I read it in high school—"Maude Miller," by John Greenleaf Whittier. It's a long poem about two people who meet, are attracted to each other, but neither does anything to build a relationship. Both go through life regretting that lack of action.

One of the final stanzas contains these words:

For of all sad words of tongue or pen, the saddest are these:
"It might have been!"[17]

Wouldn't you feel better to say at the end of your life, "I tried," than to say, "If only I had...?"

Is it possible that *you* have stories to tell the world, teachings to inspire others, and words to encourage the fearful and isolated?

You can focus your energies on all the reasons you can't or shouldn't write. Or you can say, "I have things to say. I have to write them."

And who knows the effects of your words?

---

[17] In the public domain.

- Write to find out who you are.
- Who you are determines what you write.
- The more you write, the more you learn who you are.
- The more you learn who you are, the better you like yourself.
- The better you like yourself, the more you're able to help others.

▪ UNLEASH THE WRITER WITHIN. ▪

APHORISMS FOR WRITERS

1 ▪ I write to find out who I am.

2 ▪ I write because it's my gift. The more I write, the more I know who I am.

3 ▪ If you focus on being different, how can you be true to yourself? And if you're not true to yourself, who are you?

4 ▪ I may never fully know the real me, but I search for my true self. I learn many lessons on the journey.

5 ▪ I am conceited enough to write. I am enthusiastic enough to believe I have things to say.

6 ▪ The better I know myself, the better I write. The better I like myself, the better writer I become.

7 ▪ My inner critic can be my friend, so I honor and trust that voice.

8 ▪ I write creatively, and I edit analytically.

9 ▪ I use my gifts to help others. I also give to others what I want to receive.

10 ▪ I work hard at my craft. I don't always get inspired, but I finish my work.

11 ▪ I can't make the flow happen, but I can be prepared to embrace it when it does.

12 ▪ The more I know who I am and like who I am, the truer my writing voice and the more faithfully I honor that voice.

13 ▪ My voice expresses who I am. It waits for me to discover and embrace it.

14 ▪ I find my voice through understanding others.

15 ▪ I learn from other writers. I grow my voice by paying attention to the writers I like to read.

16 • My daydreams teach me what's important to me. My first task is to pay attention to them.

17 • When I'm blocked, I listen quietly and compassionately. My deeper, inner voice wants to tell me something—something I need to know.

18 • I am committed to move deeper into myself, no matter how painful.

19 • I feel afraid when I bare my soul. I run the risk that others will despise me, ridicule me, or ignore me. But that's who I am. That's all I have to offer.

20 • When I write from within, I put into words what others think but cannot say.

21 • I want to be the best me I can, so I follow my natural rhythm, and don't try to imitate anyone else.

22 • I've spent much of my life being like others. Now I want to spend time being like the real me.

23 • Moving out of my comfort zone is right when it's the next best step, or if it fits within my superior mode.

24 • If I evaluate my writing, I compare my older work with my newer so I can see my growth.

25 • I can resent others for their achievements, or I can admire them for what they've accomplished. I can determine to work as hard as they do.

26 • I am a passionate person. I can be a passionate writer if I choose.

27 • This is the best I can do at this stage of my development.

ACKNOWLEDGMENTS

I owe so much to those who nudged and encouraged me in those early days of writing: the late Charlie Shedd, Dick Ray, Victor Oliver, and Ben Johnson.

From the Scribe Tribe that I led for nine years, I learned invaluable lessons and especially appreciate Marion Bond West, Charlotte Hale, and Evelyn London.

At the top of my list stands Shirley, my wife, who has always believed in me; my agent, Deidre Knight, who has encouraged me; my assistant, Twila Belk, who takes on all the grunt work so I can write; and David Morgan, my non-writing friend, who listens to my ideas and responds compassionately.

I've worked with many good editors over the years whom I appreciate. I'm especially grateful for the friendship of Nick Harrison, who is my friend more than my editor.

ABOUT THE AUTHOR

CECIL ("CEC") MURPHEY can't recall when he didn't want to write. Although he tried to get published first at age 16, he had nothing accepted until he was 38—"only after I'd learned a few things about the publishing industry," he says.

After Cec sold at least 20 articles, he made a double commitment to God and to himself: to never stop learning and improving as a writer, and to do whatever he could to help other writers. Thus began a lifetime commitment and passion to share with other writers what he's learned along the way. *Unleash the Writer Within* is his passion and legacy to all writers in the trenches.

Since his writing career launched, Cec has written or co-written more than 120 books, including the *New York Times'* bestseller *90 Minutes in Heaven* (with Don Piper) and *Gifted Hands: The Ben Carson Story* (with Dr. Ben Carson). His books have sold millions of copies, been translated into more than 40 languages, and brought hope and encouragement to countless people around the world.

Cecil Murphey enjoys speaking for churches and for events nationwide. For more information, or to contact him, visit his website at **www.cecilmurphey.com**.

Cecil's blog for male survivors of sexual abuse: **www.menshatteringthesilence.blogspot.com**.

Cecil's blog for writers: **www.cecwritertowriter.com**.

For more on *Unleash the Writer Within* and Cecil Murphey:
www.oaktara.com